TROPHY HUSBAND

TROPHY HUSBAND
A SURVIVAL GUIDE TO WORKING AT HOME

STEVE BREWER

UNIVERSITY OF NEW MEXICO PRESS

ALBUQUERQUE

Dedication

To my family—Kelly, Max, and Seth—

an endless wealth of material.

Acknowledgments
Thanks to everyone at the *Tribune* who've helped to make The Home Front possible: Terri Burke, Scott Ware, Phill Casaus, Louise Kutz, Jan Jonas, Melissa Jaramillo, and many others. Special thanks to Luther Wilson and Frank "Mr. Hammerthumb" Zoretich.

Library of Congress Cataloging-In-Publication Data

Brewer, Steve.
Trophy husband : a survival guide to working at home / Steve Brewer.—1st ed.
    p. cm.
ISBN 0-8263-2920-9 (cloth : alk. paper)
1. Husbands—Humor   2. Househusbands—Humor.   I. Title.
PN6231.H8 B74 2003
818'.5407—dc21

                            2002010180

Design by Melissa Tandysh

CONTENTS

Introduction   *1*

CHAPTER 1. The Zen of Working at Home, or Are You Ready, Grasshopper?   *5*

CHAPTER 2. How I Became a Trophy Husband: The Inspirational Story of Finding Redemption in Clean Socks   *8*

CHAPTER 3. Successful Telecommuting 101, or Is It Safe and Tax-Deductible to Plug a Computer and a Cuisinart into the Same Outlet?   *14*

CHAPTER 4. A Memo from Headquarters to Those Who Work at Home   *25*

CHAPTER 5. Deadlines and Buzzwords: Managing Your Home-Based Career   *28*

CHAPTER 6. Dr. Dustbunny, or How I Learned to Stop Worrying and Love the Broom   *40*

CHAPTER 7. A Man Wears the Pants in the Family, Even If They're under an Apron   *55*

CHAPTER 8. So You Don't Know Your A:/Drive from a Hole in the Ground   *71*

CHAPTER 9. Rearing Children, or Beware, Here Lie Monsters   *83*

CHAPTER 10.   My Dog Ate My Homework and My Sprinklers
117

CHAPTER 11.   Home Repairs, or Who's Been Monkeying with
My Wrench?   128

CHAPTER 12.   The Great Outdoors: You Mean There's Life
Outside the House?   141

CHAPTER 13.   Taking Care of Body and Mind, or Better Living
Through Napping   153

CHAPTER 14.   Around the Calendar, or School's Out *Again?*
163

CHAPTER 15.   Conclusions, or, Is It Time to Update My
Résumé?   183

Introduction

More than 20 million Americans now work out of home offices, tethered to the rest of the world only by our modem cables. We chose this isolated way of life to escape the hassles of neckties and commuting and coworkers who snore.

The cost of working at home is high. We spend our days buried in paperwork, a phone to each ear, a child on each elbow, a dog humping one leg. We have many responsibilities and never enough time. We always seem to be driving somewhere, just as soon as we find our car keys. It's a chaotic, haphazard, sticky-jelly-fingers way of life. And everyone I know wants to try it.

Women fought for centuries to escape the isolation of the house and get out into the parallel universe of careers and lawsuits and balloon loans. Now, they (and their men) are fighting to go back home, where they can work by themselves.

A thorough examination of this societal shift reveals why perfectly sane adults abandon decent offices to spend all their time elbow-deep in dirty dishes. It's the same reason that sociologists use to explain every cultural transition: It's the Baby Boomers' fault.

Among Baby Boomers, dual-career couples became the norm. At the same time, Boomers (who want it *all*) wanted to have children and a traditional home life like they saw on *Leave it to Beaver*.

Many couples concluded it was more efficient for one spouse to work at home. Their lives were already far too busy. Why not double up some of the demands? Surrounded by computers and fax machines and children and jelly sandwiches, the work-at-home spouse can maintain family values while still contributing to a high-technology economy.

At least that's the cover story. In truth, telecommuting gives Baby Boomers a way to wear sweatpants all day.

Every day is Casual Friday when you work at home. No, worse than that. Every day is a chore-filled Saturday, a time for old college T-shirts and mismatched socks and sturdy shoes to cushion aching feet as you race around the house, chasing pets and putting out fires. At home, you dress every day as if you're about to do some work up on the roof.

Of course, the home-office trend goes far beyond mere sweatpants. Working at home is all about freedom. We want to create our own work environments, set our own hours, produce at our own pace. We want *Oprah* breaks. We want to bake brownies during business hours and have them all eaten before the kids get home from school.

Working at home means that:

- We can shape our own schedules. (Most folks find that the hour before lunch is a good time to actually do some work—unless a deadline is looming. Then, three o'clock in the morning looks pretty good, too.)
- We can cut the daily commute out of our lives so we can spend more time driving our children to soccer games.
- We can keep tidy houses while still functioning at our computers and fielding calls from headquarters. This is why most telecommuters have baskets of laundry next to their desks.

Women, with their multichannel brains and their cool efficiency, seem more suited to the daily maelstrom of running a business at home. But now millions of men have home offices and an estimated half-million identify themselves as househusbands. This nontraditional model poses a threat to an already unstable society and to all garments labeled "Dry Clean Only."

Most Boomer men received no training in housework when they were growing up. Mom did everything. Now, in a middle-aged rebellion against the dreary workaday existence that ensnared our fathers, we're *becoming* our mothers. And we're simply not qualified.

Men used to be able to disguise their ineptitude, back when they trooped off to work and the women stayed home. We men seemed capable and aloof, out there in the trenches. Wives didn't know that much of our workday was centered around the water-cooler or that coworkers shook their heads sadly at the mention of our names. All the women knew were whatever lies we told them, and that we brought home a paycheck each week.

Now, however, men are moving their jobs home, thanks to modern technology, flexible hours, and an economy that rolls right along—regardless of whether anyone shows up at the office. We yak on the phone, slurp French Roast, and swap e-mail jokes—generally accomplishing as little as we did before. Only now, we're neglecting the housework as well as our corporate duties when we play Tetris at our desks.

A man might escape his employer's scrutiny, but there's no hiding the fact that he goofed off all day when the Little Woman comes home to the Big Mess.

Becoming a househusband is a big adjustment and requires men to think in new ways. For instance, it's difficult for a man to concentrate on preparing a nutritious supper when ESPN is showing a twi-night doubleheader. It's hard for a man to keep his self-respect when he's down on his knees on a sodden carpet, staring into the business end of a toilet, a look of grim determination hiding the fact that he knows absolutely nothing about plumbing. And it's hard to get any work done when children are running through the house, flicking boogers at each other and chanting, "Uranus is gaseous!"

Yes, it's tough duty on the home front, but you men out there can learn to master it. Oh, there will be days when you long for a necktie and a cubicle. Or, at least, a watercooler. But if you work hard and pay attention, you can become a model househusband, one your wife can show off with pride at office parties. Women will *ooh* and *aah* when you flex your knowledge of stain removers. Other men will envy your tan. And the rest of the time, you can be a hermit, a woolly denizen of Greater Sweatpantsia.

I've worked at home for more than five years now, and I've learned about plumbing and taxes and laundry and roofing tar. I've learned how to handle the stress of working alone, setting my own goals, keeping the household together and the kids out of the emergency room.

I've shared my findings in a weekly column called "The Home Front," which appears in the *Albuquerque Tribune* and other newspapers around the country. And now I've collected those observations in this book. Altogether, the following chapters make (*attention, IRS—Deduction Alert!*) an Expert Guide full of Handy Tips that could help you, the Consumer, decide whether to Try Working At Home and, better yet, Survive It.

So, study this book carefully. Recommend it to all your friends. Give copies to loved ones for holiday gifts. Together, we can start a Movement, one of capable people working at home, of harried parents banding together, of men learning to cook.

Most important, we can sell lots of these books, so that I don't have to give up being a hermit and get a real job.

1.

The Zen of Working at Home,
or
Are You Ready, Grasshopper?

If you're thinking of starting an at-home business, you must first check your mental readiness. Can you work productively without adult supervision? Do you panic when faced with unstructured time? Are you too attached to your necktie, your coworkers, and your salary to leave your workplace behind?

It takes years of mental and financial preparation to work at home. Only the strong of mind and spirit (and wallet) can withstand the daily onslaught of housework and home repairs, computer crashes, and culinary catastrophes.

Here's a handy quiz to test your mental preparedness. Think of it as a checklist of your coping resources, similar to those inventories of canned goods kept in bomb shelters. The test is self-scoring. There are no wrong answers. If you're honest with yourself, you'll soon realize you're as crazy as a loon to even consider leaving your regular job.

Question: The thing I fear most about working at home is:
(A) solitude
(B) forgetting the niceties of social interaction, such as table manners
(C) creeping insanity
(D) my children
(E) all of the above

Question: The thing I would most enjoy about working at home would be:

    (A) solitude

    (B) setting my own schedule

    (C) smoking at my desk

    (D) *Jerry Springer*

Question: When I'm working, I like to wear:

    (A) stylish clothes that catch the eye

    (B) conservative business attire

    (C) sweatpants

    (D) nothing

Question: When the doorbell rings, I know it will be someone trying to sell me:

    (A) Avon

    (B) Amway

    (C) fresh fruit

    (D) salvation

    (E) all of the above

Question: When working on a computer, the error message I fear most is:

    (A) "Insufficient memory at this time."

    (B) "A fatal exception has occurred."

    (C) "General failure."

    (D) What's an error message?

Question: My child is stuck up a tree, screaming for help. I would:

    (A) call the fire department

    (B) climb up the tree and help him down

    (C) stand below, ready to catch him, while gently coaxing him down

    (D) hide in the house until he figures it out on his own

Question: When the phone rings, I expect it to be:
- (A) an important client
- (B) a telemarketer
- (C) my spouse, wondering whether I've accomplished anything today
- (D) the state Child Protective Services Department

Question: Faced with two inches of water on the laundry room floor, I would:
- (A) unplug all electrical appliances, clean up the mess, and try to find the problem
- (B) call a plumber
- (C) call my spouse and whimper into the phone
- (D) tell the kids we're having a pool party

Question: To make my home the perfect place to work, I need:
- (A) a supportive family
- (B) a loyal dog
- (C) e-mail
- (D) duct tape
- (E) a straitjacket

Scoring: If you're anal retentive enough to actually add up your score, you're probably not suited to working at home. At home, you're surrounded by toys, scrambled files, and dirty socks. Better that you should work in a regular office, where they have janitors.

The rest of us will plunge ahead, searching for our utopia—those rare moments when it all comes together. The kids are in school, deadlines have been met, and the dog is asleep. And our warm, fluffy sweatpants have just come out of the dryer.

2.

HOW I BECAME A TROPHY HUSBAND:
THE INSPIRATIONAL STORY OF FINDING REDEMPTION IN CLEAN SOCKS

Working at home isn't for everyone, and neither is this chapter. This, you see, is the part of the self-help book where I tell my own inspirational story. Usually, it's where the author reveals how low he stooped before he got a firm hold on his bootstraps and fell over backward into the wretch you see before you today. Celebrities tell of crimes they committed before they saw the light—that the real money is in confessions. Politicians and TV preachers describe drugged orgies in detail, call them "youthful indiscretions," then say, "Oh, but we don't do that anymore. And neither should you impressionable teens out there."

My own tale is a sordid one. It's a long and crooked climb to being a model househusband. There have been times when I've failed, oh Lord, there have been times when I've backslid, gold-bricked, and drunk beer at lunch. There has been fast food, God help me, and ice cream and that flirtation with the grocery checker with the overbite. Yes, it's a rocky road to redemption, but I finally found my salvation. I donned the mantle of House-husbandhood (say *that* three times fast) and learned to wear it well.

In keeping with our self-help format, I will now tell my own story. It's mostly for the men. You women can skip ahead rather than submit to the whiny-baby ramblings of a man who finally faced what women have known forever—bullets sing on the home front and artillery thunders in the distance, and there's God's own wrath if you let down your guard.

With vigilance, Post-It notes, and occasional snootfuls of Scotch, a man can overcome the obstacles and survive working at home. He can find his redemption in a child's laugh or the gurgle of an unclogged toilet. He can create his own little Margaritaville and still maintain the pose that he is an asset to the community.

Here's my story.

I started working at newspapers when I was eighteen years old, which means I remember when newsrooms had manual typewriters, cigar smoke, and chattering Teletype machines. Most of the Linotype operators were deaf, and this one scary old lesbian had only nine fingers, but she could set type faster than a speeding bullet. Copyboys smoked dope on the roof and forgot what they were supposed to be doing. Trash cans occasionally caught fire. This is the world I grew up in, and I inhabited it until I was forty. Computers came along during my career and reporters started wearing Dockers and all smoking moved outside to the loading zone, but the atmosphere of newsrooms—the daily rumble of butting heads and sarcastic asides—remained much the same.

When I was about thirty, I started trying to write fiction. My wife and I—then child-free—were living it up in San Francisco, where we both worked in the news business. Something about all that fog and Dashiell Hammett's lurking ghost moved me to attempt to write mystery novels.

Fiction gradually took over my life, though I mostly worked when everyone else at my house was asleep. I lived a strange, vampiric existence, cooped up in the sunless pre-dawn hours, sucking down java and pounding at the keyboard.

By the time I was facing my fortieth birthday, I'd published four novels, but still worked at a newspaper in my adopted hometown of Albuquerque, New Mexico. I was slipping into the standard midlife crisis over what I really wanted to do when my wife surprised me with this: leave the newspaper. Write full-time. Work at home. She'd be the steady income and I'd get a chance to pursue my dream.

(Great birthday present, huh? Hard to top that one, though I will say that she got a new job *and* a weekend in Las Vegas when she reached a similar crisis point a few years later.)

My birthday gift came with conditions. How can you dump one income without a lot of conditions? One was that I would take over all household chores. We bid fond farewells to our cleaning lady and our yard guy, canceled our sons' after-school care, and I became a househusband.

I eased into my new responsibilities as I recovered from the shock of moving from a bustling newsroom to a dusty house. I drifted around in my bathrobe, pausing occasionally to plunk at the computer before surrendering to the temptation to nap. Pretty soon, the place was an unholy shambles. I'd let cobwebs and dustbunnies and Power Rangers and other vermin take over my home. Probably my lowest moment came one day when I was nearly asphyxiated by a whiff of my boys' bathroom (their motto: "Whaddaya mean, 'aim'?"). I could no longer neglect cleaning. I needed to learn how to do it properly and regularly, so that we could stand, so to speak, to use the same bathrooms again and again. You can't just move every time the bathrooms get disgusting, though I seem to recall that it worked when I was a bachelor.

I buckled down, got my house in order, and managed to keep it that way. And I still got my writing done, despite the many distractions of the household and the untold hours of struggling over computer games in which I saved the universe from evil aliens.

Like a lot of stay-at-home dads, I cut myself off from the world. I became a modern-day Robinson Crusoe, shipwrecked in a land of laundry, lawn work, and America Online. Since my men Friday are both under the age of fourteen, I lost touch with working adults. For me, an extended adult conversation became, "Would you like to Super-Size that?" Sometimes, even that question stumped me.

I've disappeared from the radar screens of my friends and former coworkers. I stay indoors all day, sitting at my computer, jumping up occasionally to run around frantically and scrub stuff. I drive the kids to and from school, muttering about traffic.

If I see neighbors, I duck my head and hurry back into the house. I'm a solitary man, living inside my head rather than out in the real world, having conversations and pretending to be normal.

That's a third of my life. Another third, if I'm lucky, is spent in bed. The last third of the pie is the slice that's been dropped on the floor. That's the time when my two sons are home with me, when I'm a full-time dad. That "quality time" is what sends so many fathers screaming back to the old workplace. Back to, say, newsrooms, where your colleagues were adults, more or less, and where you once spent eight hours a day safely out of your children's reach.

Becoming the perfect househusband is not easy, friends. Temptation is strong and ESPN is on twenty-four hours a day. A romp in the park with the dog is more seductive than slaving away at the desk. Bars are open during school hours. For you who want to follow my path, know this: You must teach yourself discipline. You must have determination. You must sacrifice. You have to get down on your knees, friends, to scrub a toilet the right way, especially if there are young boys in the house.

I'd had a good example set for me. Until my mother started a career when I was fourteen, she was a stay-at-home mom in rural Arkansas, a member of the Busy Bees Homemakers' Club who won ribbons for her baked goods at the Grant County Fair. She had two boisterous sons, a house to clean, meals to prepare, and a garden to ignore. I seem to remember that she was always tired. Now I know why.

I'm home all day every day, just as my mother was. I have two boisterous sons. I bake from mixes. My house is sometimes presentable, but my dog-cratered lawn resembles the surface of the moon. My neighbors think of me as the strange guy in the bathrobe who always keeps to himself.

My wife comes home from a hard day at the office full of career news, gossip, and lamentations, and I find I have little to say. How did my day go? Quickly. What did I do? Lots, though you can't tell it to look at the place. What did I think about all day? Um, chores.

No wonder my stay-at-home mom retreated to the comfort of soap operas and coffee klatches whenever she got the chance. At least she heard some adult dialogue; she might glean something interesting to recount later. My guilty indulgences are computer solitaire and crossword puzzles. What can I report, that I scored 720 against that dastardly computer, or that I learned a new word for an Asian goat? Somehow, these do not make topics for extended conversation. I worry that I'm letting myself go. When it all got to be too much for my mom, she'd repair to the comfort of bare feet and loose housedresses, skipping the makeup and the curlers. I wander around in cutoffs and sandals, unwashed and unshaven, grazing the fridge, smoking cigarettes, and scratching myself.

Despite the slide in my appearance, my wife certainly enjoys having a houseboy to call her own. She likes not having to lift a finger around the house, even if it means that she comes home to a cave dweller who can't put together a complete sentence.

My sons love having a parent around all the time, but I suspect it's because I'm becoming one of them. I pepper conversations with terms like "poopy," and "monkey-butt." I think a snappy retort is a singsong, "I know you are, but what am I?" The kids take me for granted, just as I did when I was boy and my mom slaved to keep us clean and well-fed. Another lesson women learned long ago is that the parent who spends the most time with the children is the one most easily ignored. The kids tune out the frequencies of our voices.

When I'm at my wit's end, sweating over a broken faucet, and the boys are pillaging the house like little Vikings, the last resort comes bursting out: "You guys are in a lot of trouble! Wait until your *mother* gets home!"

Most of the time, though, I manage to keep an even keel. I've found a rhythm to working at home. My office is a comfortable, alluring place so close at hand that I can sneak in some work while the kids watch TV. I do my writing while still keeping the entire family in clean socks. Occasionally, something occurs that's unexpected and fun. It's not all drudgery. In fact, it's a sort of bliss, once you've got that multitasking rhythm going.

CHAPTER TWO

That "flow" is why some workers thrive at home like hothouse tomatoes. They drive minivans and attend school assemblies and run million-dollar corporations off their kitchen tables. If you think you could be one of those stay-at-home dynamos, then you should turn immediately to the next chapter, in which I show you viewers at home how to set up your Tax-Deductible Home Office and Begin to Take Full Advantage of its Financial Benefits.

3.

SUCCESSFUL TELECOMMUTING *101,*
OR
IS IT SAFE AND TAX-DEDUCTIBLE TO PLUG A COMPUTER
AND A CUISINART INTO THE SAME OUTLET?

Many two-income couples have an annual discussion about the possibility of one spouse working at home—at tax time. One of them will throw out the idea that it would be more economical to lose one income and pay less in taxes. Then these couples laugh hysterically and go back to filling out their 1040s. Every year at tax season, financial experts urge Americans to use the annual bloodletting as a time to take stock of household spending, withholding, and income. And every year, across this great country of ours, we taxpayers, relieved at having met the deadline, respond by saying, "Pass the tequila!"

So, I encourage you to take a few minutes now—while the Infernal Revenue Service isn't breathing down your neck—to consider the advantages and drawbacks of having one spouse work at home.

A lot of misinformation on this topic regularly gets spread through the national media like fertilizer, resulting in sprouting hopes and an ever-growing number of Americans who believe that working at home will produce a bountiful harvest of financial rewards. Not the least of which is digging themselves out of the hole caused by taxes. The Tax Foundation reported recently that a typical, two-earner family in 1998 lost nearly forty percent of its income to federal, state, and local taxes, more than the family spent on food, clothing, and shelter combined. Take away one of those incomes, and the tax burden diminishes greatly. Artful dodgers can even find ways to lose money on their home businesses every year, which can reduce the amount the salaried spouse pays to the feds.

But, you say, the family has jettisoned an entire income. How can even a substantial reduction in taxes make up for that loss? Heh-heh, I reply nervously, you've got me there. Beats the heck out of me. I'm no financial expert. My wife takes care of the money at our house. I can't even remember my ATM number. However, financial experts such as my wife would bear me out when I say other, not-so-visible savings occur when one spouse opts to work at home. Let's look at some of them.

COMMUTING

If the work-at-home spouse no longer drives across town to a job, then less is spent on gasoline and maintenance. Even reduced wear and tear on the vehicle can be factored into the formula, though this requires knowledge of calculus. At-home workers soon realize, however, that we end up driving just as much, chauffeuring kids to school and to after-school events. Not to mention driving to the supermarket, the hardware store, the dry cleaners, the doctor's office, the dentist's office, the mental health clinic, etc. . . . .

Okay, maybe those savings aren't so great. Let's try something else.

FOOD

Lunches out are costly, and entertaining clients can be even pricier, especially if one of them is a guy named Buck who expects to procure his weekly alcohol consumption with your credit card. By working at home, you can prepare light, nutritious meals for mere pennies a day. Of course, it rarely works out that way. With no formal lunch hour, you graze all day long, resulting in overall higher grocery bills as well as the cost of larger sweatpants. In fact, you can spend as much on your daily allotment of Chee-tos as you did previously on fancy lunches. And eating alone can be a drag. Before long, you may find yourself inviting Buck over for a beer.

SUPPLIES AND FURNISHINGS

Everything you buy for your home office—down to the last paper clip—is tax-deductible. And that provides opportunities for the creative worker. If you can prove your business required you to invest in many expensive gadgets for your home office or to visit, say, Tahiti, then you stand to reap a financial boon come tax refund season. The problem with this strategy is that you must actually spend the money first. You can gallivant around, throwing your money away, but only a small portion will later be saved in taxes. And the folks at MasterCard will still want their money.

CLOTHING

Aha! Now here's one that certainly should be recorded in the category of "Money I don't have to spend anymore." Employers expect their workers to meet a certain dress code. If the job you're leaving is the type where you're expected to wear a suit every day, you certainly should save money by working at home. T-shirts are cheap. You may find, however, that you destroy more clothes at home than you ever did at the office. Little tasks you do around the house—chores you would've paid someone to do when you had a full-time job—have a way of eating clothing. A weed-whacker, for instance, can reduce your favorite jeans to confetti in no time. And medical bills may result as well.

So there you have it. A pragmatic look at the numbers provides proof positive that most couples can benefit financially by having one spouse work at home. At least until the auditors catch up to you.

GETTING STARTED

Okay, let's say you've examined your financial status and your mental preparedness and you still delude yourself that working at home is a great idea. Subtract from the equation any extraneous considerations, such as the proximity of the refrigerator to your desk at home. Still want to try it? Sure I can't talk you out of it?

Damn.

Well, then, it's only fair that you be properly prepared. The first step toward a successful home business is setting up an efficient office. Needs vary, depending on the type of business and personal preferences, but some general rules apply. For instance, you will need more space than you think. And you may want doors that lock, particularly if there are children in the house.

Even smallish homes have underused areas that can be converted into office space. Breakfast nooks, closets, attics, garages, even a corner of the bedroom can be reconfigured for business use. Remember, however, that your family may not adjust well to the change. If you section off a piece of a family room for your office, your kids may still think that's where they belong when they're watching cartoons. Adding a wing or a second story can give you plenty of room. But do you really want to invest in such expensive remodeling before you know whether your home business will be a success? I didn't think so.

Once you've determined where to put your office, you'll need basic furnishings. A solid desk and a comfortable chair are the bare minimum. And you'll need a computer, naturally. Hardly any business operates without one these days, and computers offer endless opportunities for distraction and procrastination. You'll need file cabinets, though milk crates can do the job if you're operating on a shoestring. A work table is nice, too. I recommend an old door suspended over the file cabinets. That way, you won't feel much of a loss when it collapses under the weight of unfinished paperwork. Lighting should be appropriate for the workspace. Bright enough to see what you're doing, but dim enough so that you don't notice the dust that has settled over everything. A sofa makes a pleasant addition to the workspace, especially once you become accustomed to regular siestas.

After properly furnishing your office, you'll be broke. That should serve as a good impetus for working your ass off and making your home business a success.

One final note: get separate phone lines for your business phone and computer. You don't want to keep an important client waiting while your kids are calling the neighbors to ask whether their refrigerators are running.

MYSTERIES OF THE EAST:
ARRANGING YOUR NEW OFFICE

Proper arrangement of the home office can be critical to productivity, so many people who work at home turn to the ancient art of feng shui.

Feng shui (pronounced "fung shway," from the Chinese for "I tripped over my wastebasket") is based on the notion that proper arrangement of furniture, mirrors, fountains, and other gewgaws for sale at exorbitant prices, can channel the life force, or "chi," that flows through us and our homes. According to feng shui principles, improper arrangement can stifle creativity, impede productivity, dampen your chances of success, and generally make you feel like a heel by surrounding you with negative energy. Good placement of furnishings can attract success, place your work life in its proper context, and give you long, lustrous hair.

So, right away, even the uninitiated can see that feng shui offers unlimited potential for ripping off gullible consumers such as yourself by providing a pseudo-religious solution to your messy office. This principle is known as "hoo-ey."

Not all feng shui practitioners are full of "hoo-ey." Many are dedicated to improving the lives of others for a lucrative hourly rate. A feng shui consultant typically will examine your workspace and make suggestions for removing clutter and placing particular objects in ways that will bring the most cosmic benefit. By hiring a consultant and carefully following the recommendations, you can improve your own well-being while also contributing to the growing New Age economy, known as "ka-chiing."

Of course, not all of us have "moo-lah" lying around to invest in feng shui consultants. For those at-home workers on a budget, we recommend the following do-it-yourself approach.

Clutter is the enemy of the smooth flow of "chi." Allowing clutter to proliferate in your office can result in confusion and misplaced invoices and poor self-esteem, a condition known as "moo goo gai pan." Your first step toward a balanced life should be to throw out all the papers that clutter your filing cabinets and to get rid of any toys, sports equipment, nail clippers, dishes, and dirty socks that have found their way onto your desk. Once all clutter is removed, you can go on to the second step, which is to dig through the trash in search of those really important papers you threw out. This step is known as "fung me."

The next step is to determine your various compass points. For this, we recommend that you use, well, a compass. Different directions carry different forces. For example, northwest is your travel site, west is your creativity site, and southeast governs wealth. Then, using an octagonal map called a "bagua chart," easily obtainable off the Internet, you can determine how to align elements (wood, water, fire, uranium) and colors to direct the flow of positive energy through your home office. Sure, this might require you to relocate everything in your office, but won't it be worth it if your "chi" is properly aligned? You'll feel better almost immediately, though you won't be able to find anything.

You may need to add some decorator items to your home office. For instance, feng shui often uses round mirrors to deflect bad energy and direct good energy. Some items, such as bamboo flutes, crystals, seashells, goldfish bowls, indoor fountains (collectively known as "junk"), can be purchased from Internet feng shui sites for only twice what they'd cost at Wal-Mart.

Desks should never face a wall, as mine does, because it blocks the flow of energy and makes you feel "lo mein." If space is too tight to set your desk facing out, then place a mirror above your computer so you can spot anyone sneaking in the door behind you. That way, you can see them coming and clear erotic e-mail off the screen faster than they can say "bruce lee."

The color red can stimulate you and your fame, while green, properly placed, signals health and growth. This is why many feng shui experts recommend leaving your Christmas tree up year-round.

These are just basics, of course. If you want to really improve your "chi," then you should seek expert assistance. Look in the Yellow Pages under "bilk me."

PROPERLY DECORATING
YOUR HOME OFFICE

I have chattering teeth on my desk. Not just your standard, plastic, chattering teeth. These have big, pink feet attached. The whole thing hops around while the teeth chatter. Worth a smile the first thirty times I saw it. After that, I tried to ignore the little gizmo, which sent me telepathic signals all day: "Wind me up. C'mon, it'll be fun."

Where did this laugh riot come from? I have no idea. I assume one of my sons set it here, then forgot it.

Desks collect toys, gimcracks, gewgaws, and freebie calendars, whether they're squatting with their mates in some big office or all alone at home. Such is their nature. If zoologists traced it back far enough, they'd find an evolutionary branch where four-legged desks split from the same primitive species that spawned the packrat.

In large offices, workers decorate their cubicles to demarcate their personal spaces and to show off their toys or family photographs. You can tell a lot about people by the artwork, cartoons, and accessories they keep on their desks. For instance, a person who uses a ballpoint pen with a large pink plume attached tends to be the fun-loving sort. A man whose desk is covered with photos of dogs, but no people, might seem shy at first, but he'll be loyal and friendly and will respond well to praise. A bowling trophy indicates a heightened appreciation for healthy activity and beer.

Desk decoration can also be a warning flag. I've never gotten a satisfactory answer from a secretary who had Garfield prominently displayed. Never enter into a conversation with a man who keeps on his desk a photo of his boat.

Some items are silent protests against the Powers That Be. Is there any cubicle in North America that doesn't sport a "Dilbert" cartoon? I once worked with an unhappy woman who kept a plastic lamp on her desk. The lamp was shaped like a mushroom cloud and had a red bulb inside. When her superiors walked past, she'd flick on the light and say under her breath: "Boom. Heh-heh-heh." We were all secretly glad when she moved away.

In a home office, you can decorate your work space any way you like. It won't matter anyway. Everyone else in the household will consider your desk a holding area for their own junk. Soon, even that inspiring photo of your smiling spouse will be buried beneath old magazines and underwear.

In a single week, along with the chattering teeth and the usual mail, I found the following on my desk: a round plastic rock, a stuffed Roswell alien (twice), several Transformer beasts in various stages of mutation and undress, six shoes, two yo-yos, four Super Balls, a chocolate heart left over from Valentine's Day (how did I miss that?), seven Hot Wheels cars, a toy dump truck, two Koosh balls (don't ask), a dead flower, nine coffee cups, three Beanie Babies, and thirty-seven dirty socks. I didn't want any of these things on my desk. I prefer a clean, organized work space. But detritus moves through, and the magnetic desk picks it up.

The problem is worse at our house because of our dog. He picks up toys and other items around the house and chews them. He's trained us to pry the item away, praise him for handing it over, then put the item on a horizontal surface out of his reach, such as my desk. He then fetches up another item and we do it all over again. As the numbers show, he's particularly keen on dirty socks. I think the dog sees it as his way of cleaning the house. He finds stuff on the floor, brings it to me, and I eventually put it away. He's just trying to help. And I'll keep doing my part, cleaning off the desk for the next inevitable accumulation—but I'm keeping the chattering teeth.

TO WORK AT HOME
YOU NEED A LOTTA STUFF

Internal Memo
Marketing Dept.
Megalotta Office Stuff Inc.

Comrades:

As you know, we've made terrific progress in capturing the market of people who work out of their homes. This growing market of suckers has resulted in booming sales at our 236,405 huge retail warehouses nationwide.

To remain competitive, however, we must always be on the lookout for new ways to persuade America's workers to buy doodads for their home offices. We must convince these workers they *need* our products. This memo will outline some possible strategies. We here in Marketing thought we'd run them up the flagpole and see who bends over. We look forward to your input.

RECEIPTS

Our itemized receipts have been very popular with at-home workers who use them for tax purposes and to seek reimbursement from their customers. But we can do more to help our clientele. From now on, all sales of our popular computer games software, such as "Flight Simulator," will read out on cash register receipts as "Envelopes."

PAPER SHREDDERS

Here at headquarters we know most offices don't need a paper shredder. What's so secret that these workers need to shred? What are they, the Pentagon? But paper shredders have proven to be hot sales items. The customers buying these shredders are what we here in Marketing call ASUEEs (All Stocked Up on Everything Else). The ASUEEs are a fickle market and soon will move on to something else—probably DVD drives. Therefore, we must find ways to quickly move these shredders. We propose an advertising campaign highlighting the benefits of confetti. One can never have too much confetti on hand. What if a party breaks out? And there's always the possibility a ticker-tape parade might pass by your window. We think this approach will sway those fence-sitters who still haven't purchased a shredder.

SOFTWARE

Our Technology Department is in the process of developing a new suite of home-office programs that will allow the average at-home worker to draft documents, store files, send e-mail, create charts, do illustrations, keep accounting records, send faxes, and figure out taxes, all without ever leaving the chair. We believe the new Deluxe Home Office Suite For Idiots 2002 will be a "must-have" for techno-geeks who work at home. Naturally, the new suite will be incompatible with all existing operating systems. But our Technology Department is working up a new operating system that will retail for only $249.99. Plan for the Christmas rush now!

HEADSET PHONES

These items, which clip right onto one's head and leave the hands free, are proving very popular with home-office types, particularly those who like to pretend they're pilots while playing "Flight Simulator." Display them prominently and move 'em out!

THE BASICS

We're not forgetting our root market here. We know most people shop Megalotta Office Stuff Inc. for the basics—paper, pens, clipboards, staplers, file folders, etc. The problem with many of these items is they last too long. A shopper buys, say, a stapler for his home office and he's set for life! He'll never need another stapler. And one box of a thousand staples will last years. This doesn't produce the high turnover we want. We need our customers to walk through the door every week, so they have an opportunity to ogle the latest product offerings, such as paper shredders. Therefore, we have redesigned most of our basic items and are now manufacturing them out of the finest Indonesian plastic. File shelves, staplers, pencil holders, even office furniture will now be constructed of this particularly brittle blend of polymers. The slightest use results in breakage. We'll still carry items made of more durable material, such as metal, but their prices will be quadrupled to encourage customers to go with the plastic. You can bet we'll see those customers again!

That's it for now from Marketing. Next week: The latest in electronic organizers!

4.

It has come to our attention that you who don't go to an office every day do not adhere to an enforceable dress code.

Granted, many of you bailed out of the 9-to-5 world to escape suits and ties. But how can you expect clients and the wider world to take you seriously if you don't dress for success? Wouldn't you feel more professional if you followed a basic dress code?

We here at headquarters have drafted a proposed dress code for those who never leave their homes to perform their valuable work functions. We will conduct an open comment period during which we'll seek your input. Then, without warning, the following requirements will become mandatory:

1. Pajamas are not proper office attire. Ditto for bathrobes.
2. Blue jeans are acceptable, of course, as long as you're not meeting clients face-to-face. But there are limits, people. Jeans worn more than six days in a row without washing will be considered a violation of the dress code.
3. Jeans with holes, tears, slashes, patches, burn marks, tire tread patterns, coffee stains, or large ink spills are verboten. Legs of said jeans should be approximately the same length.

4. Baby spit-up on your shoulder will not be considered an accessory. Dried spit-up on both shoulders cannot be passed off as epaulets.

5. T-shirts are acceptable as long as they are in good condition (see item 3 above). T-shirts should not bear beer slogans, rock band logos, curse words, or depictions of naked people. Remember: even if you don't see clients all day, you'll probably run into your child's teacher at the supermarket.

6. Sweatshirts. See item 5.

7. Sweatpants are comfortable, work-at-home attire, but wearing them in public should be reconsidered. No one's backside looks good in sweatpants.

8. Underwear should be laundered regularly. Turning it wrong side out doesn't count.

9. Flannel shirts are proper attire if you're a lumberjack. However, we recognize that many of you work in poorly heated spaces and therefore need to layer on warm shirts, so we are willing to overlook these, even if they are essentially pajamas. Flannel shirts should have at least fifty percent of their original buttons. Any shirt you owned in high school probably should be discarded.

10. Denim shirts. See item 9.

11. Clothes should be put on hangers after they are laundered. Valuable work time is wasted sorting through that pile on the floor of your closet, trying to select a garment on the basis of crunchiness.

12. We here at headquarters recognize that many of you enjoy the freedom and comfort of bare feet. But hazards lurk in your home. Sharp-cornered plastic Lego. Need we say more?

13. Similarly, working in the nude to circumvent these regulations is not recommended. That coffee is hot. Trust us.

14. Personal hygiene remains important, even for those

who work alone. Here, we will refer you to the Rule of Doubles. You can safely double whatever your practices were when you worked at a regular job without risking dismissal or divorce. For example, if you showered daily when you went to the office, you can now shower every other day. Ditto for shaving. However, if you were one of those pigs who only bathed once a week to begin with, you might want to consider taking the math to the other direction.

15. Teeth should be brushed regularly and deodorant applied every day. You may be working at home, but there's still your family to consider. And, believe us, they'll let you hear about this.

There, that wasn't so painful, was it? Just a few basic rules for maintaining a professional appearance, even though no one is around to see it. You'll look better and feel better. And you'll be ready to get right to work every morning, which is all we here at headquarters care about, anyway.

5.

Deadlines and Buzzwords: Managing Your Home-Based Career

People who work at regular jobs often ask us who work at home, "What do you do with yourself all day?" This is an exceedingly stupid question. Folks in 9-to-5 jobs seem to think we home-office types have lots of time to lollygag in our pajamas and watch soap operas. This simply is not true. We perform many so-called "invisible" tasks—such as scraping lime out of toilet bowls—and those jobs take time. Most days, we barely scratch the surface of all we need to do before, whoops, it's bedtime again.

So, as a public service, to generate understanding between wage slaves and we pajama-wearing housespouses, I've drawn up a typical schedule for working at home. It will be illuminating to those who've never tried to operate a business out of their laundry room, and will show that we stay-at-home workers deserve respect and sympathy.

We'll start with a forty-hour workweek and chip away from there. Telecommuters often work on weekends, too, but including Saturdays and Sundays in our formula makes the math too complicated. You wouldn't want me to strain over these numbers and perspire on my pajamas, would you?

First of all, it's not really a forty-hour workweek, is it? Most of us can do our jobs only when the kids are in school. The period between the last bell at school and your standard five P.M. quitting time is completely lost to recountings of the school day and the usual threats over homework. So there goes around seven hours a week. We lose another hour (or more) getting the kids to and from school each week. That takes us down to thirty-two hours.

Running the washer is a task we can do while performing other jobs, but there's still all that folding and fluffing and hanging things up. For a family of four, laundry adds up to at least five hours a week. Down to twenty-seven hours.

Keeping the house clean takes a lot more time than you clock-watchers might expect. A conservative estimate is eight hours a week. And that's if we forgo non-essentials such as dusting.

Allow an average of two hours a week for medical emergencies, appointments with the doctor and/or dentist, and visits to the vet. This varies from week to week, depending on whether the children insist on climbing trees and the dog insists on eating Tinkertoys. Down to seventeen hours now.

Many housespouses are responsible for keeping the yard mowed, watered, raked, and fertilized. Another two hours a week, and another argument in favor of xeriscaping.

Grocery shopping? We'll go conservative and say we can do it in an hour, if we don't linger in the liquor department. Fourteen hours left.

We lose one hour a week fielding annoying calls from telemarketers and at least another two hours yakking on the phone with family, friends, and repairmen. Down to eleven hours.

Lunch requires an hour a day (this includes wolfing down the food, which usually takes half as long as the preparation time). Six hours left.

Answering e-mail and playing computer games might not seem productive, but it's a vital activity that keeps stay-at-home parents sane and in touch with the outside world. An hour a day—minimum—goes to keeping our fingers on the electronic pulse of the Internet and to mastering "Sim City."

What's left? One hour. And during that hour, we must perform all the wage-earning work that's accomplished each week. Is it any wonder we seem so frantic as deadlines near? Is it any surprise we end up pounding away at our computers at four A.M. on Saturdays?

Now that you have hard evidence that we are just as harried as the rest of the working world, I hope you people with regular jobs will think twice before asking a stay-at-home parent, "What do you do all day?"

You accommodate us this way, and we won't tell your boss about the hours you waste secretly playing "Minesweeper."

DEADLINES CAN BE MURDER

A kindly old editor once explained to me the facts of life in journalism: "Deadlines are simple. Cross the line, and you're dead."

Probably not an original thought, and he had a gleam in his eye when he said it, but I took it to heart. Through two decades in the news business, I rarely missed a deadline. In fact, I usually delivered my stories early. It left more time to argue with the editors.

Deadlines are more extreme in the newspaper business, but every industry has them. That's why you see people using laptop computers at the beach. It's why the businessman with the car phone melded to his ear nearly mowed you down in traffic this morning. And it's one reason ulcer medications sell so well (parenting being the other reason).

When you have no boss looming over your desk, deadlines are largely self-imposed. Granted, clients make demands and there are only so many hours in each day. But when you work at home, your schedule is your own. If you need to work all night to meet a deadline, so be it. You can catch up on your sleep when you're done. The trick is to pace yourself, so you don't pull too many all-nighters. Keep busy every day, plan ahead, and make a schedule. Stay on top of the work before it gets on top of you.

Okay, you can stop laughing now. No, really. Stop it.

Here's how to formulate your schedule: divide your work in a given week by the number of days you actually can work on it. Set daily goals. Meet each goal, and—voila!—you've met the deadline.

Stop that chortling. You think I can't hear that?

So the secret is in the planning. Remember that Monday is grocery day, Wednesday is laundry, and Friday is that dental appointment. Write it all down so you don't forget. Then chart the available hours that remain.

Enough with the snickering. I'm trying to give you good advice here.

Did you leave room for all this weekly planning? Getting organized takes time. And you'll need to regularly evaluate your plan to make sure it's working. If things go wrong, you can reconfigure your schedule. If it means doubling up your work hours for a day or two to still hit that deadline, it'll be worth it, won't it? A happy client is a client for keeps. And an unhappy client won't care that you were called away by an equally unhappy schoolteacher who wanted to discuss little Johnny's spitball habit.

There you go again. All right, forget it. I don't have time for this anyway. I've got a project to complete. And if it's not finished on time, I'm dead.

JUGGLING MANY TASKS AT ONCE—
WITH YOUR TOES

These days, the darling of the business community is "multitasking." A boss hears the term "multitasking" and he clutches his bosom and big, happy tears well up in his eyes. He loves multitasking because he thinks it means more work is getting done.

Before multitasking came along, bosses expected you to do every job they dumped on your desk. Now, they expect to you to do all those jobs *at the same time.*

Every employee now is supposed to be like a street entertainer, a One-Man Band, the guy with the bass drum on his back and the cymbals between his knees. We manage all the projects, production, and publicity all at once, playing the music and keeping time to a beat in our heads: "hurry, hurry, hurry."

Employees—with their Palm Pilots and their miniature

phones and their go-go attitudes—adopted multitasking as a way to get ahead. It soon became a competition, with everybody rushing headlong into doing everything at once—Phoning, PowerPointing, prognosticating, and whanging away at those cymbals with their knees. Before long, you'd become a second-rate employee if you couldn't dial a phone number with your toes.

But is this the best way to get high-quality work? Aren't employees all scattered and confused? Shouldn't they concentrate on one thing at a time? For answers, bosses should look to those who are the ultimate multitaskers, people who work at home offices. Not only do we do our work and manage our careers here at home, we also do the housework, the yardwork, and tend to children, *all at the same time.*

We're the pioneers in multitasking, the white lab rats in a great business experiment. And we're never "off the clock." When a kid throws up in the middle of the night, he doesn't need a cell phone to contact Daddy.

Recently, I had a light workday scheduled. My only big job was to print a 350-page manuscript and mail it. The rest was just housework, hanging out with my two sons, and a few errands in the car. Before my sons were awake, I started printing the manuscript. My printer needs to be fed more paper about every ten minutes, so I'm forced to hang around, waiting for it to make that groaning noise that means it's hungry. I could've used those hours for some quiet meditation, some navel-gazing about my career, but I chose instead to multitask. Here's how it went:

Feed the printer. Wander around the house gathering up laundry. Get the washer started. Feed the printer. Get more coffee. Take out the trash. Feed the printer. Check freezer to see whether there's anything that can be disguised as a nutritious dinner. Start grocery list. Feed the printer. Straighten kitchen and hurriedly wipe off countertops. Feed the printer. Move laundry from washer to dryer and start a new load. Feed the printer. Make two work-related telephone calls. Feed the printer. Wake children. Issue breakfast instructions. Feed the printer. Feed the dog. Feed the printer. Collapse into chair to catch my breath. Feed the printer.

By the time the manuscript was done, I'd accomplished much, but I was scattered and confused and required a nap in the early afternoon.

So, bosses everywhere, take it from we busy housespouses: multitasking may not be the best solution. It wears people out, and an exhausted, frazzled worker is an accident waiting to happen. You might be better off treating each employee less like a One-Man Band and more like a member of an orchestra. Let each play the lead sometimes, but let them rest sometimes, too.

Otherwise, you'll find your employees dialing phones in their sleep. With their toes.

BUZZING YOUR WAY TO SUCCESS

Business loves buzzwords. These days, new words buzz their way into the language every day. Even people who have no connection with dot-coms find themselves spewing the geekspeak of computers and corporations. Pretty soon, the buzzwords become so common that people apologize for using them. For instance, every time someone uses the term, "thinking outside the box," now, it's followed quickly by "forgive the expression." People recognize that "thinking outside the box" has become hackneyed. I won't be surprised if they're soon looking for a way to crawl back into that box, wherever it is.

This is what I call the "bunny ears" phenomenon. Remember, a few years back, when everyone would make those little quote marks in the air with their fingers? By using finger quote marks, they were showing they were hip to their own triteness and were being ironic. After a while, whenever I saw air quotes, I wanted to form my own fingers into a "V" and poke someone in the eyes, a la The Three Stooges.

Those of us who work at home are somewhat insulated from the business world (in particular from the wealth it generates). But this distance means that we're often "out of the loop." We'll hear a term such as "unwinding the stack" and have no idea what they're talking about. This can be damaging to one's career, particularly if one sometimes comes in contact with 25-year-old business hipsters who toss these terms around willy-nilly.

Using a little imagination, we can assign meanings to the buzzwords, meanings that apply to the work-at-home world of laundry and looming deadlines. To wit:

Outside the Box. Anywhere toys are found when they haven't been put away, i.e., everywhere.

Out of the Loop. The dog has escaped his leash and is romping around the neighborhood, menacing joggers.

Unwinding the Stack. Separating the whites from the colors on laundry day.

Taking It to the Next Level. Carrying the laundry upstairs.

The New E-Conomy. Someone has too many hyphens. Apparently, you can put "e-" in front of anything to indicate that it has to do with the Internet (which, you'll notice, doesn't start with "e"). I recently saw a reference to "e-friends," which I assume means people you've never actually laid eyes on, but have only communicated with via e-mail. We lonely at-home workers should take advantage of this easy way to look modern and businesslike. You can put "e-" in front of anything. For example, you could say, "I'm taking my e-car to pick up my e-children from their e-school."

Virtual. Another computer term, meaning not quite real. Proper usage: "It's a virtual certainty that I will be late picking up my children."

Mission Statement. A credit-card bill you can't afford to pay, which gives you reason to work harder.

Re-purposing. Using any product in a way that violates

its design intent. Cutting the bottom off an empty bottle of bleach and using it to bail water from a flooded basement, for instance, is "re-purposing." Sounds more businesslike than "jury-rigging."

Comfort Zone. Anywhere the children aren't.

System Integration. Dresser drawers that shut properly.

Brand-building. Wal-Mart.

Paradigm Shift. The hours you work between sundown and dawn. Proper usage: "My virtual deadline means I've been pulling the paradigm shift all week."

The "Vision" Thing. What you're missing when you can't find your eyeglasses.

Stock Quote. "Moo."

Streaming Data. What the plumber uses to explain the sound of running water under your house.

Napster. A work-at-home parent in mid-afternoon.

Empowerment. What you get when you learn to use buzzwords in your daily life.

NEED MOTIVATION?
CHECK YOUR FEEDBACK

One problem with working at home is that you don't get enough feedback.

But wait, you say, isn't that the whole reason to work at home? *Less* feedback? For most people who work in regular offices, less feedback from their bosses would seem like a gift from heaven.

Sure, many of us who work at home made the move to escape bosses breathing down our necks. But now that our necks are largely boss-free, we find that we struggle without some response, some validation that we're doing a good job.

Working alone means never having to say you're sorry. It means no one cares whether you goof off all day, as long as you get the work done eventually. It means you don't have coworkers giving you nonverbal cues, rolling their eyes when you do something stupid, or impatiently clearing their throats when you spend too much time on the phone, gabbing with your friends.

Without feedback, it's sometimes hard to get motivated. Why bust your hump meeting a deadline when no one will notice? Why waste time with filing when a nice big heap of paperwork does the job just as well and nobody will see it anyway? Why bother to clean the house when the kids will just mess it up again, anyway? Such goldbricking can lead you to worry all the time, though. When you're your own boss, you keep wondering whether you should be breathing down your own neck. And is that even physically possible?

We at-home workers have to supply our own feedback, just like we have to do everything else around the home office. We give ourselves motivational speeches. We develop tools that will make us stay busy, that will validate the choices we've made.

There are ways to tell whether you're doing a good job, ways to pump yourself up for the next task. Here are a few you can try.

Make to-do lists. Nothing is quite as satisfying as scratching a line through a chore, relegating it to the category of "finished." Naturally, there's a temptation to pad such lists. If you find yourself checking off "getting out of bed" and "lunch," you might want to re-examine your goals.

The Stuart Smalley approach. Look in a mirror and tell yourself that you're good enough, smart enough, etc. . . . Warning: prolonged staring into a mirror can quickly degenerate into a search for wrinkles, zits, and nose hairs. And you don't want those activities on your to-do list.

Every time you complete a task, do high-fives with imaginary coworkers. Or, you can train your dog to give you a low-five whenever you need a boost.

Try the methodology used by behavioral psychologists: punishments and rewards. When you do a good job, reward yourself in some way. I recommend ice cream. When you waste the whole day, berate yourself and withhold the ice cream. Bet you do better tomorrow!

When you're really in desperate need of feedback, call on your family. Your children will be only too happy to give you reasons to perform better. Most of these reasons center around the need for expensive new sneakers. If you ask your spouse for assistance, make sure your to-do list is hidden out of sight. Otherwise, count on it getting a lot longer.

Saving the best for last, I've got one sure cure for the motivational blues. If you think your career is going nowhere, that you're suffering from a lack of feedback from appreciative coworkers, then go look at the place where you keep incoming mail. There will no doubt be a stack of bills there. If that doesn't get you up and moving, then maybe working at home isn't for you. Maybe you really do need a boss breathing down your neck. But bill collectors provide all the feedback most of us will ever need.

MAINTAINING SELF-ESTEEM WHILE PRETENDING YOUR CAREER IS ON TRACK

All right, let's say you've established your home office. You've decorated it. You've got phone calls coming in and work going out. You've learned the Joy of Sweatpants. Now let's talk about self-image.

Most working people have simple job descriptions. Presented with a blank for "employer," they write a name and address and go away satisfied that they've done their duty.

For folks who work at home, it's not so straightforward. When it comes time to fill out a form, the blank spaces become paralyzing philosophical queries into what we do and where we're going with our lives. I've often fallen into such black holes of self-analysis. Within minutes, I'm ready to return to a regular job, any job, rather than ponder how I surrendered my manly provider role and became a househusband. I sit at my desk, repeating a mantra until the bleak depression passes. The mantra goes like this: "Would you like fries with that?"

Sometimes, even the mantra is not enough. When it gets

really bad, I go to my closet and stare at the dusty neckties hanging there, leftovers from the days when I worked in a newsroom. That's usually enough to snap me out of it, to remind me of why I chose to stay home and eke out a living rather than enjoy the comforts of a regular salary and benefits package. But it's an uneasy peace. All it takes to send me into a mental sputter is to have someone ask, "And what do you do for a living?"

The latest fit of navel-gazing was sparked by an alumni questionnaire from my alma mater, the University of Arkansas at Little Rock. The journalism department regularly asks alumni to update their personal data so it can send out newsletters that show us how our old classmates have become more successful than us. I suspect the school also uses the database to hit us up for money, which is laughable, considering that most alumni are journalists or worse, people so poor that their idea of a charitable donation requires asking a bum for a receipt.

The questionnaire has ominous blanks for the following: Business address and phone number, Current position, City where you work, Employer, City where employer is located (if different). It also has spaces that say, "Check below if applicable: New employer. Promotion with same employer."

All fine and dandy if the alumnus has a regular job. But the categories don't measure the accomplishments of those of us who work at home. No questions about "Loads of laundry done per week" or "Number of months without a trip to the emergency room."

Sure, I have a job, of sorts. Under Current Position, I can write *author and newspaper columnist.* That sounds pretty good, though they'll catch onto me once I list the same address and phone number for Home and Business. And what do I list under Employer? Myself? The honest answer probably would be my two sons. They boss me around more than anyone else.

When I get into these self-absorbed funks, my career as a writer starts to look like a financial sinkhole and I can't even consider it a real job. Instead, I consult my Inner Woman and focus on the rewards of the man-hours I put into the household—

reasonably well-adjusted children, a happy wife, a sometimes-clean house, a business wardrobe built around sandals and flannel shirts.

If I want to be truthful on the questionnaire, I should answer *househusband* under Current Position. I can imagine my old classmates snorting at that. But you can bet your ass the school wouldn't ask me for money anymore.

Househusband, however, just doesn't sound glamorous or interesting or fulfilling. It doesn't reflect how hard I work or how well my job status fits with my wife's career and our domestic demands. It doesn't say: here's a guy who's striving, one who's making a splash. Here's a guy whose wife is proud of him, even though he is officially unemployed.

So I came up with a different job title. It may leave my classmates scratching their heads, but it'll make me feel better when I receive the newsletter in the mail. Current position? *Trophy Husband.*

6.

Dr. Dustbunny,
or
How I Learned to Stop Worrying and Love the Broom

A friend gave me a pillow embroidered with this message: "My idea of housework is to sweep the room with a glance."

I heartily endorse this philosophy. Apparently, I'm not alone.

Sociologists at the University of Maryland have found that nobody's doing much housework anymore. In a national sample of nearly 15,000 people over 30 years, the researchers found that the average housework load per adult dropped from 17.5 hours per week in 1965 to 13.7 hours in 1995.

For women, the averages have dropped even more. Women averaged 30 hours per week of household drudgery back in 1965, when most worked in the home. By 1995, their workload had plummeted to 17.5 hours. Men averaged only 4.9 hours of housework per week in 1965, but that climbed to 10 hours per week by 1995.

Women (even those with full-time jobs) still do the lioness's share of the housework, the study noted, but Americans generally are just doing less.

"One speculation we have," one researcher said, "is that perhaps this is not a highly valued activity."

How's that for mastery of understatement? I'd like to put it more bluntly: given our busy lifestyles, we choose to live like pigs.

In most families these days, both parents work, just to make ends meet. We finish the workday dead tired, only to rush off to after-school activities, dinner parties, and church functions. Home computers mean we work or answer e-mail after the kids are in bed. For many of us, any spare time is spent flat on our backs, recuperating, while we zap through inane television shows with the remote control. We're too beat to worry about housework.

And yet, the housework never goes away. Laundry piles up. Meals must be prepared. Floors get gritty. Cobwebs magically appear.

The only answer is to ignore it all. Put it off. We delay the laundry until our colleagues sniff and make faces when we pass in the hall. We hold off on grocery shopping until the kids are eating leftover lasagna and drinking root beer for breakfast. We teach the children not to write "dust me" on the furniture with their fingers. If they complain about cobwebs, we tell them we're preparing early for Halloween.

We procrastinate as long as we can, trying to make it to the weekend. Then we try to cram 27.5 hours' worth of housework into Saturday.

This is the way we live in the modern, high-tech society. Like pigs.

At my house, I do perhaps 90 percent of the housework. That was part of the agreement when I bailed out of a regular job to work at home. My wife works long hours. I'm here all day. It *should* be my job to do the cleaning. I put off the housework just like the rest of you, even though I'm surrounded by it all day. I get distracted by pursuits that are more interesting. And let's face it, *anything* is more interesting than housework.

All our friends and relatives know I'm in charge of keeping the place clean, which is why I panic when we get one of those phone calls that says company's arriving in fifteen minutes. I've got a reputation to protect. I zoom around the house like The Flash, snatching up dirty clothes and wiping crumbs off countertops and slamming bedroom doors. Sometimes, I can fool our guests into thinking the house looks nice. But I watch them carefully. I don't want them opening a closet door by mistake or—God forbid—looking under a bed.

For many two-career couples, housework becomes a waiting game. Whoever can't stand a dirty house has to do something about it. The reason that men still average less housework than women is because we tend to have a higher tolerance for filth. Look under a bachelor's sofa sometimes. Brrr.

"Maybe men's low level of housework will become the norm with both men and women deciding: 'This is not how I'm going to allocate my time'," the researcher said. "Maybe women are becoming more like men."

A terrible thought, to be sure, especially for guys. Already, we don't know how to play our gender roles anymore. Things have changed since we grew up. Workplaces have become sanitized, smoke-free, no-cussing zones, very different from when men ruled the corporate world.

Now, as more men flee that world in favor of working at home, we're being forced to pay attention to housework. Guilt is the main motivating factor here. Our wives go off to their hard-charging jobs, slaving through long hours and deflecting the chicanery of coworkers, and we feel bad if we don't pull our weight at home.

But it's difficult to maintain an aura of stony masculinity while prancing around the house with a feather duster. Men have to find ways to make housework interesting, efficient, strenuous and, well, *manly*.

Men love to solve problems and make decisions. It makes us feel competent and masculine. Most men would rather spend two hours figuring out an exotic labor-saving method for doing a job than the five minutes the actual job would've taken if done the old-fashioned way. Especially if the new solution involves power tools.

Fortunately, technology offers many options for a man with a credit card and the will to master working at home.

I write my columns on a computer, which delivers them to newspapers all over the country without me ever leaving my chair. Simultaneously, machines are washing my clothes and my dishes. A machine that sucks the dirt off my floors would be operating, too, but the kid who was running it went off to play basketball. Thanks to the marvels of telecommunications, I could at any second talk with anyone around the world, though it'll most likely be a chat with the doctor after my son takes the basketball in the kisser again.

Microwave ovens are the salvation for men who cook or whose coffee is cold. Self-cleaning ovens are a boon to all mankind. And where would we be today without the TV remote? Jumping up to change the channels, that's where.

Smart, at-home workers learn to take advantage of all of these technological advances, so we can perform more than one job at once. Doubling up is the secret to success. We wear many hats, but most of us only have one head, so we must use that head to keep a look out for life's little efficiencies.

Here are some examples:

- Never walk from one room to the other with empty hands. Pick up toys, magazines, dirty socks—anything—and carry them along with you. You can put them where they belong, then carry something else in the other direction. Eventually, the house will be picked up, even if you can't remember why you originally started going from room to room. And those aimless miles you've walked can count as your exercise for the day.
- During warm weather, you can water your lawn and bathe the dog simultaneously. This works until the dog gets smart enough to find that one spot on the lawn where the sprinklers don't reach.
- Don't sit still while talking on the telephone. You can shelve books, set out something to thaw for dinner, load the dishwasher, and even dust while chatting with friends or clients. Note: this only works if you have a cordless phone. Otherwise, all your conversations center around the topic: "What was that crashing noise?"
- Use a catch bag on your lawn mower. You can trim the grass and pick up autumn leaves at the same time. Leaves that drift into corners where you can't reach them can be designated as mulch.

- Always load the dishwasher while cooking. Otherwise, you're standing around, waiting for water to boil, and that's not efficient. If you leave the dishwasher standing open, you can put in the pots and pans and spatulas as fast as you dirty them. By the time the meal's over and the table's cleared, you've got a full load and can start the machine. A word of warning, however: you probably will need one item—a particular skillet, a colander, a slotted spoon—to finish cooking the meal. That item will be in the dishwasher already, and it will be dirty.

- When sorting laundry, try to lump together the clothing that goes to particular closets. For example, I usually wash my clothes separately from those that belong to my two sons. That way, when my clothes come out of the dryer, I can fold them and hang them up without making side trips to my sons' rooms. It saves steps. It also keeps whatever might be hidden in the kids' pockets—Gummi Bears, for instance—from getting all over my clothes. If you use this method with towels, however, all the towels end up in one bathroom. People in the other bathroom soon find themselves drying off with toilet paper.

- Always summon a child to help when you're sweeping. They're down there close to the floor, anyway. Why should you have to bend over to reach the dustpan?

- You can wipe down the counters in the bathroom while brushing your teeth; after all, you're only using one hand to brush. Why not keep that other hand busy? If you need both hands to brush your teeth, you have worse problems than dirty countertops. You might want to use one of those hands to dial up a dentist. Make sure to use a cordless phone.

I hope these little tips help you to manage your household in an efficient manner. Remember: every minute saved on household chores is another minute you can spend at your desk, playing computer games.

A MODEST PROPOSAL

To leaders of all the countries in the world: let's pull together and repeal the law of gravity.

What's gravity's attraction? Gravity is holding us down. Think how much easier life would be without it. People would be happier if they could float freely, without gravity in their lives. And it would be heaps easier to get up off the sofa.

Much of housework consists of battling the effects of gravity. Everything ends up on the floor. I spend hours each week picking up the big stuff and vacuuming up the small stuff.

I started paying attention to gravity after I became a father. When you have kids, gravity works overtime at your house. Every time a kid lets go of something, it becomes another victim of gravity. The kid sees nothing wrong with this. Children actually prefer all their worldly possessions spread out on the floor, easy to see, handy for whatever whim whams them next.

When they were younger, my sons were The Spillage People. So much food and drink ended up on the floor that we had to get a dog.

These days, the gravity at our house appears to be strongest just inside their bedroom doors. My sons stagger in under the weight of their backpacks and jackets until they're just inches inside their rooms, then everything falls. I call this area of rich gravity the Drop Zone.

Naturally, we couldn't repeal gravity altogether. If we did, all of us would go spinning away into space, and I don't think we want to go that far, even if it means no more housework. But perhaps we could get gravity to ease up somehow.

For instance, toys would be a lot easier to gather if they were all floating waist-high. I could dance lightly through the room, plucking them from the air as if they were flowers and stuffing them into a laundry basket.

There would be kinks to work out. What if all the dustbunnies floated in the air at nose height? That's no good. We'd all be too busy sneezing to enjoy our own new sense of lightness. Or, what if gravity was relaxed just enough so that our shirts always floated loosely around us? Some of us aren't intended to expose our midriffs.

What we need, I suppose, is selective gravity. Gravity that we could control. Then we could get toys to float into the toy box while the dustbunnies stayed in the corners where they belong. We'd be lighter on our feet, but not so light as to bump against the ceiling all the time like helium balloons. This would be ideal.

My sons and I were talking about gravity recently in the car. (We spend many hours in the car. They think I'm their chauffeur.) We decided that the perfect situation would be if you were surrounded by a "bubble" of gravity that you could control with your mind. By slightly shifting the gravitational pull within your bubble of influence, you'd be able to move at will, even fly.

This, naturally, would make you one helluva superhero. The boys decided we'd name such a hero Gravitron. He'd soar through the air, battling bad guys, knocking them over with his gravity bubble or flattening them to the ground by increasing gravity's pull on them. He'd wear purple tights, because that's what superheroes wear, and also so he wouldn't have to worry about his shirt floating up and exposing his belly.

If he wanted to work as a house cleaner, Gravitron would be on the gravy train.

It would be even better if flexible gravity was universal. What if we all could control our immediate gravitational fields? Wouldn't the world be a better place? We wouldn't need fossil fuels anymore. We could zip around freely, our gravity bubbles like bumper cars, without gravity's friction and oppression.

I hope you scientists and politicians out there will get right on this. We need anti-gravity if we're going to keep getting up off the sofa.

And since I've mentioned it first, I'd like to coin a trademark for this wonder and claim a share of all future royalties. Here's what we call the opposite of gravity: hilarity.

GIVE BLOOD:
WORK AROUND THE HOUSE

I recently sliced my finger while opening a jar of pickles. You might have trouble picturing anything less sharp than a jar of pickles, but this one had some little rough spot at the rim and it snagged my middle finger and gave me a bright, inch-long gash.

No big deal, right? Didn't even hurt much, though it bled as if I'd run it through a jigsaw. It was, however, a reminder of the dangers of working around the house.

They don't tell you this when you sign on to do the housework. You think, sure, there'll be a lot more to do if I work at home—car pools, cooking, and cleaning—but "bleeding" isn't part of the job description. You don't expect that your new fashion accessory will be the Band-Aid.

Homes, our cozy nests, are dangerous places. They're full of knives and power tools and wet tiles and electric wires.

Working around the house, it's possible for a klutz like me to get hurt most every day. The day after I started sporting a Band-Aid for the pickle slice, I pinched my pinkie in a TV antenna, peeling back a sweet little butterfly of epidermis. Another Band-Aid, same hand. I looked like an offensive lineman—tape on every finger.

The wrist of the same hand was nearly healed from an incident a few days earlier. I was playing fetch with our dog and he forgot the whole "throwing the ball" portion of the program and tried to snatch it out of my hand with his teeth. Maybe he didn't want to be the only one in the family without an opposable thumb.

So that's the story on one hand up to the wrist. Usually, the rest of me bears a similar spattering of cuts, scrapes, and bruises, proving that life is perilous for house hermits.

I should've known it would be this way. My past performance in any sort of household labor has shown a predilection toward injury.

Years ago, when I was a bachelor, I was cleaning up the aftermath of a party, my hand down a garbage disposal to fish out a beer-bottle cap, when my then-girlfriend flipped on the "light" to help me see. The disposal didn't actually cut off any of my fingers, but it sure made them wish they'd been elsewhere. The relationship with the girlfriend went south soon after. And I've been flinchy about garbage disposals ever since.

Every plumbing job I've ever attempted has resulted in barked knuckles or worse. I can't handle a hot skillet without touching it somewhere. "Some assembly required" should be the slogan scrolled above the door of the emergency room.

Even something as fluffy as laundry can hurt. Inside the door of the dryer? There's that sharp little latch . . .

And these are just the external injuries. Inside the body, all those muscles, tendons, and ligaments are just begging to be stretched, strained, severed, spindled, and mutilated. I once walked like Quasimodo for a week because I bent over awkwardly to pick up a book off the floor. Recently, I squatted over a broken sprinkler head so long that my legs seized up. I thought for a moment I'd have to do the Chuck Berry duckwalk everywhere I went.

Okay, now you're thinking: quit your quacking, you big baby. Most working stiffs would gladly risk the injuries to stay home all day. You're right, of course. Working at home—without several layers of bosses lining up to breathe down my neck—is worth the hazards. I wear my Band-Aids with pride.

At least now that my kids are older, the Band-Aids are the "flesh-tone" variety. It was hard to impress the fellas down at the hardware store, to show them I'm a man's man who troubleshoots his own household repairs, when I wore Barney the Dinosaur on every finger.

COOKING MADE EASY: IT'S CALLED "TAKE-OUT"

With more of us guys working at home, it's becoming more common for us to be put in charge of cooking meals. This is a grave mistake in most cases, one that could lead to outbreaks of nutrition-related ailments like rickets and scurvy.

I speak in generalities here and the usual exceptions apply. I know at least two couples of which the guy is a gourmet chef and does most of the cooking. But most guys seem to be missing the cooking-nutritious-meals gene. Apparently, it's in the same DNA strand as the stopping-to-ask-for-directions gene.

The problem isn't that cooking is so hard or that guys are too lazy to do it right. It's just that guys are like dogs: to us, pretty much everything is food. If you can eat it, it must be good for you. And the easier it is to get, the better.

This was built into our genetic code during the caveman days, when men went around foraging for things to eat. Men would wander the wilderness, picking up things and sticking them in their mouths to see if they tasted good. It was mostly a matter of trial and error. If a rock broke out Trog's teeth, then Trog wouldn't eat any more rocks. If Trog found a dead animal, he'd gnaw on it and take it back to the family because it was good.

It was just a short step up to Trog going around killing animals for the family to eat. I suspect he got tired of waiting for roaming animals to fall over dead from old age. He had to take matters into his own hands.

But it was the woman in this scenario, I believe, who discovered that meat held over a flame got even tastier and was less likely to give the Trog family a screaming case of trichinosis. Mrs. Trog was left back at the cave, whittling new teeth for her husband, and she had time to experiment with the food he brought home. It was Mrs. Trog who learned which foods tasted best together and which ones kept the family healthy. It wasn't long, I suspect, before she was demanding a spice rack and a kitchen island.

Trog, meanwhile, was still out there hunting and gathering. Being a guy, Trog would eat almost anything while he was on the road. This mentality, which eventually would lead to the proliferation of fast-food joints along our nation's highways, allowed Trog to eat new and different foods, including those forbidden by Mrs. Trog. And that, ladies and gentlemen, is how pork rinds came to be.

A modern guy still carries around those Trog genes. Left to

his own devices, he will forage for food rather than plan a well-balanced meal and prepare it. Why cook when Taco Bell has a drive-thru window?

When a guy is forced into cooking, he will produce odd combinations, many of them involving beer. And he still wants an element of danger in the process, which is why barbecue grills are so popular.

If you doubt these generalities, check with most any bachelor. When I was a single guy, I started thinking about dinner the moment I got off work. No advance planning, no thawing something ahead of time. I got in the car, picked up fast food and zoomed home to eat it before it got cold. My refrigerator was stocked with condiments, Pepto-Bismol, and a few mystery leftovers that would stay safely wrapped in aluminum foil until a biohazard team happened by.

Now that cooking is part of my job description, I've learned to prepare simple meals and—most importantly—make good use of the microwave. "Heat and eat" is my middle name. But foraging still is in my genes. My best cooking tool is a car.

GROCERY SHOPPING FOR GUYS: THERE'S MORE TO THE STORE THAN BEER

Among TV commercials, this one rings the most true. Two slacker dudes are in a store with limited money, trying to decide between beer and toilet paper. They choose the beer, then respond in unison to the question, "Paper or plastic?" We laugh not just at the follies of youth or because we've been in similar straits ourselves. We laugh because they're *guys*. Buying groceries. And we all know what a hoot that can be.

Supermarkets don't cater to men. The logic of the layout escapes us. The competing brands, colorful labels, and computer pricing are confusing. We don't care about comparison shopping. In fact, we don't like shopping at all. We like buying. And we want it all to be finished quickly.

If supermarkets were designed for guys, they'd offer one type of each product, labeled generically in black and white: "Beer," "Chips," "Cereal." We wouldn't even care what was inside the boxes, so long as we could just grab one, throw it in the cart and move on to the next. If we got home with a box marked "Cereal" and it turned out to be corn flakes rather than organic, Honey-nut Prune-de-Ohs, that would be fine. If it turned out that all the boxes contained beer, that would be even better.

I took a course in college called "Industrial Psychology." One of the marketing strategies we studied was supermarket layout. Store designers intentionally put the things you need most often—milk, meat, coffee, beer—in the far corners, so you must pass all those loudly labeled products to buy the staples. They're hoping you'll buy things you don't really need at inflated prices. Guys fall victim to this syndrome, which is why corn chips and canned chili are now considered food.

This knowledge has come in handy as I've gradually mastered grocery shopping. My secret is that I always go to the same store, even though it's miles away from my home. It's a smaller market and I've learned where everything is kept. I can do a week's shopping there in less than an hour, zooming up and down the aisles like a contestant on "Supermarket Sweep."

Here are some other tips to help guys do the family shopping:

- Don't waste time selecting the best shopping cart. They all have one wheel that goes waga-waga-waga. Just take one and go.
- Buy whatever's cheapest. Forget brand loyalty, family favorites, or what might make a lovely dinner a week from Tuesday. Buy lots of cheap stuff. Fill the cart with it. Later, in the kitchen, you can piece together the different products into something resembling a meal.
- Some supermarkets recognize the "buy cheap" philosophy and cater to it. Those are the markets that sell those tiny boxes of detergent only good for one or two loads. Guys—especially bachelors—buy those little boxes,

even though they cost only pennies less than a big box. This means much of the laundry will be done soapless, of course. Eventually, all the clothes will be a uniform gray and you can eliminate detergent from your shopping list altogether.

- Make excuses. Guys famously refuse to ask directions, which means they can wander up and down supermarket aisles for days, holding their tattered lists, searching for the one item their wives insisted that they buy. You can avoid this problem with a simple answer when you get home: "I forgot." This will lead to a certain amount of eye-rolling and an even lower opinion of guys in general and you in particular, but it will save time.
- Get the eggs last. No matter where the supermarket Easter bunnies hide the eggs, make that your final stop. Then you can set the eggs on top of everything else and they won't get crushed. Until the bag boys get hold of them. They'll put them in the sack with the beer and the motor oil—you can have an omelet as soon as you get home.
- Don't be too hard on the bag boys when this happens. They're guys.

"DRY CLEAN ONLY" IS FOR SISSIES

It was a simple blue shirt. A camp shirt, I think it's called, with a flat collar and buttons up the front. My wife picked it up during a shopping excursion, but it was a lesser purchase, not one that gets immediately modeled for the family. It was the type of shirt that goes into the laundry for softening and then an initial wearing days later, when she could check if I was alert enough to say, "Is that a new shirt?" Unfortunately, that day never came. She never got to wear it.

I noticed the shirt when I was doing laundry. It still had the sale tags on it, so I dutifully removed them. Then I read the

"Washing Care" label, which seemed to have been written by someone with an inadequate grasp of English. I remember noting that the shirt was a synthetic material, Mylar or Pylon or something, as I tossed it into a pile of like colors and dumped it into the washer.

When I removed that load from the dryer, I intended to hang up the shirt so it would be unwrinkled for its maiden wearing. I pulled it from the tangle of hot clothes and found it was much smaller than it had been when purchased. I mean, *much* smaller. You expect a little shrinkage with a new item, but this shirt was half the garment it used to be.

My wife took the surprise with equanimity, as she does most household mishaps.

"It was on sale anyway," she said, which somehow made it all right.

We gave the shirt to my older son, who was pleased to have it and didn't even care if it buttoned the wrong way. A happy ending, right? But the shirt wasn't through. The next time I washed it, it shrank some more. And it has continued to shrink each time it goes through the laundry. The younger son's wearing it now, and it won't be long before the shirt becomes doll clothes.

Work-at-home spouses automatically become the laundry mavens in two-parent households. Laundry's one of those jobs we can do while we're working on other things. We drop what we're doing every thirty minutes or so and trot over to the washer and dryer to move another load through the process. But when the work-at-home parent is a man, disaster awaits. There's something about laundry that evades men, which is why you see so many of us going around in pink tube socks.

Most men subscribe to a philosophy best summed up as "More is better." If the washer will comfortably hold five towels and two shirts, why not ram in six towels, three shirts (they're getting smaller all the time), and all the socks and underwear you can find? Slip a little extra in each load and you've eliminated a whole load, maybe two, from that day's labors.

If the underwear comes out an unlikely pastel, who cares?

Nobody's going to see it, anyway. If everything comes out wrinkled, so what? That's what steamy bathrooms are for. Hang up a shirt while you shower and, by the time you put it on, it's damp, but wrinkle-free.

All of which is fine if you're doing laundry only for yourself. But shrink a kid's favorite ratty T-shirt and you're going to hear about it. And when you add women's clothing to the mix, the situation is ripe for catastrophe. Manufacturers make women's clothing out of exotic fabrics in bleeding colors and with elaborate fasteners that catch on everything. It's all part of the conspiracy to get women to buy more clothes. Run those babies through the wash a time or two and they're goners.

Especially if a man is at the controls.

7.

A Man Wears the Pants in the Family, Even If They're Under an Apron

When I was a teen, my mother always took care to never brag about her salary. Her career was taking off, and there were times—thanks to bonuses and the like—when she threatened to make more money than my dad. This would not do. She knew that my father prided himself on his role as family breadwinner, and she suspected it would damage him somehow if his wife started winning more bread. So she soft-pedaled her whole career, always making it sound as if her growing income was so much butter-and-egg money, stashed in the cookie jar.

My, how times have changed. These days, it's the men who brag about how much money their wives make. The most important necessity for men who want to work at home is a wife who earns a hefty chunk of change every week.

Many men have trouble making the adjustment. We've been socialized to base our worth on the size of our incomes. We want to flaunt our large, manly paychecks, to wag them under the noses of lesser men. We're conditioned to want expensive toys, such as Porsches and Rolexes and titanium golf clubs. We want women to see us as desirable mating prospects (even if we're not in the dating pool anymore) and we foolishly think the size of our wallets matters.

One of the grim realities of the movement toward working at home is often a plunge in income. Telecommuters who move their existing jobs home from the office may not experience this, but the rest of us, those who take a flyer on a whole new career, must expect a certain amount of paycheck shock. When a man bails out of the corporate world to start a dot-com business or (God forbid) a writing career at home, he essentially has chosen unemployment. No matter how hard he works, his income suffers, at least in the short term, and this can affect how he feels about himself as a man.

Soon, he may find himself deferring to his wife on all household decisions, particularly those that involve money. She's making the money, she should get to decide how it's spent. And you can bet titanium golf clubs won't be high on her list.

It's not just money, though. Men defer to the wage-earning spouse for the same reason traditional housewives let their husbands make all the decisions back in the "I Like Ike" days. They want home life to be pleasant for their hard-working spouses. Better to give in than to argue every little decision. The corporate spouse gets enough of that crap at the office.

Deferring all the time can be dangerous. Eventually, you get into the habit of letting your wife decide everything. This will make you stupid. Before long, you can't make any decision without a consultation with her. You find yourself uttering inanities such as "Does this shirt go with these pants?" or "Can I go out and play with the guys?" A man can even surrender so much of his household authority that he ends up in a completely different house. To wit:

After I'd been a househusband for a couple of years, my wife (envious of all my "free" time at home) announced that she needed a vacation from her high-stress job. Our two sons were in school, so we really couldn't travel anywhere. She said she'd happily spend the time off at home and perhaps engage in some "retail therapy." Fine by me. I was starting a new novel, so I could hide at my computer all day while she galloped around shopping malls to that immortal battle cry: "Cha-a-a-arge it!"

The first day, she bought a new bed. Our twelve-year-old bed was in bad shape because the boys regularly used it as a trampoline. So many of the springs were broken, it was like sleeping on a bagful of elbows. My wife bought the biggest bed she could find. Again, fine by me. I'm a big guy and I need room for my nocturnal thrashing. But the bed took up so much space in our small bedroom that we could barely walk around it.

The second day, she bought a puppy. Once again, fine by me. I'd held out for years, citing lawn damage and chewed shoes as reasons to skip pet ownership. But no argument holds up against "Boys need a dog when they're growing up" and I'd already surrendered. We named the puppy Elvis, partly as homage to my Southern roots and partly because it's fun to say, every time he goes outside, "Elvis has left the building."

So, we're sitting around our tidy little house, admiring our giant bed and speculating that Elvis will be one whopper of a big dog when he grows up, when the phone rings. It's our real estate agent, who announces that she's found us a new house.

Now, we didn't want a new house, not really. But as the boys grew larger, we'd started half-heartedly looking around. We'd put so many restrictions on the search—price range, size, space for the home office, particular neighborhoods—that I wasn't too concerned about the real estate lady turning up anything. Boy, was I wrong. She'd found us a house all right. Wrong neighborhood. Way too expensive. Twice the size of the house we currently occupied. No separate office. But as soon as we drove up to the house, I knew we'd buy it. It was a good deal and my wife was in a spending mood.

Work on the novel sputtered to a halt, replaced by paperwork, worry, home inspections, and deal-making. Within a month of first seeing the new place, we were moving.

Of course, we had to have new furniture for rooms that didn't even exist in the previous house. A formal dining room, for instance. Separate living room and family room. My wife and I bounded through various stores, buying things willy-nilly, accompanied by the background music of ringing cash registers.

One of the purchases was a new desk for my home office, which now occupies one end of the family room. When my office was separate from the house, tucked away in its own cozy building, it didn't matter that my desk consisted of an old drafting table and that my dusty bookcases were jammed with yellowed manuscripts and notebooks. But now my office is right here in the house for any visitor to see. So I got this nice, cherry-veneer desk with a hutch, drawers, and cubbyholes, perfect for hiding the accumulations of paper that accompany being a writer. And a small table for the printer. And file cabinets. And dust-free bookshelves for reference works. And it occurred to me that two years after abandoning life in a regular office, I ended up building myself a cubicle.

All this because my wife felt ready for a change. I wanted none of these items. And I sure as hell didn't want to go through the trauma of moving. But once the woman becomes the chief breadwinner, the man gets into the habit of saying, "Yes, dear." (I got my revenge once my wife finally called a halt to all the changes that shook up our lives. I sneaked around and talked to her boss and we agreed: no more vacations for her.)

THE DOCTOR IS IN . . .
MY HEAD

Good afternoon, doctor. Should I just lie down over here? Forgive me if I'm a little nervous. I've never been in psychoanalysis before, but I understand how it works. I've seen all of Woody Allen's movies, so I feel like a veteran of the couch.

My problem? Getting right to the point, eh? Not interested in hearing about my childhood first? My fear of snakes? Okay, okay, the reason I'm here is, well, I'm starting to worry about my masculinity. There, I've said it. Now, I'll just be going . . .

All right already, don't get your goatee in a knot. I'm back on the couch. Yes, my masculinity. You heard me right. I don't stutter, Sigmund.

What? Am I angry? No, I'm not angry. Just uncomfortable. This is a tough subject to discuss.

It all began when I became a househusband. I'm a writer and my job, such as it is, can be done at home. My wife and I have two sons, and it only made sense that one of us stay home to handle school transportation, summer vacations, and housework. I gladly took on the role.

Yeah, the housework. Why are you giggling? Men can do housework, if pressed. It's not that hard to keep a clean house, as long as no one looks behind the furniture. But we're getting off the topic here. As I was saying . . .

What? No, I don't wear an apron. What kind of crack is that? All my clothes are dotted with grease stains because I refuse to wear an apron.

No, I don't have an "issue" with aprons. Do you want to hear my problem or not?

Okay, so I've been a househusband for a few years now and overall it's going fine. But my career still isn't as lucrative as it should be. And housework gets to be a repetitive drudge. And my kids drive me crazy and . . .

No, I can't just go back to work. First of all, I don't want a regular job. Second, we've arranged our lives around having one spouse at home, tending the children, the house, and the lawn. Even if I wanted to go back to a regular office, it wouldn't be possible.

But I worry about whether I'm still a Real Man. I'm not the main breadwinner in the household and that makes me feel inadequate. I feel guilty because my wife works so hard while I'm hanging out at the swimming pool with my sons.

Okay, those may be normal responses, but other things really bother me. For instance, I find myself taking an aberrant interest in home decorating. I never used to care about that stuff. I find myself thinking about supper first thing in the morning—what should I thaw, what vegetables go with what entree. I'm troubled by dustbunnies and cobwebs. These aren't manly obsessions.

Hobbies? I have a few, but they're not the type Ernest Hemingway would pursue. It's not like I could take up hunting or something. Can you imagine my kids' reactions if I came home with Bambi strapped to the bumper? And physical activity of any kind seems redundant after a day spent mowing and vacuuming.

Mm-hm. Yeah. Sure.

That's your advice? Remember that a man's worth isn't determined by his paycheck? Why don't you just have that done up as a needlepoint sampler and hang it outside your door? Save me a hundred bucks an hour.

No, I don't do needlepoint, you jackass. One more crack like that and I'm going to exercise my masculinity on your head.

Sorry, sorry. I guess I've got a lot of pent-up aggression.

Yeah, I could treat my stay-at-home career more like a real job. Maybe that would help. Maybe it would distract me from the demands of the household and help me to focus on the work that actually earns some money. Then I'd feel more fulfilled.

What's that? I might even want to wear a necktie? In my own home? Are you kidding?

I'd rather wear an apron.

"HONEY, I HATE TO BOTHER YOU AGAIN, BUT . . ."

Here's a tip: you're calling your spouse at the office too often if the receptionist recognizes your voice before you get past "Hello."

With no coworkers to natter at all day, we stay-at-home parents tend to snatch up the phone with the least provocation. We speed-dial our spouses to consult, to complain, to commiserate. Every scraped knee, every development with a client, every household "emergency" such as minor flooding merits a quick call.

What, you might ask, is wrong with that? It's part of the marriage contract that we share everything, right? Wrong. Your spouse is busy earning a living. He/she is in meetings, making decisions, or pumping out paperwork. If you call frequently, your spouse will get distracted and become as unproductive as you. This is not the best approach to job security.

But how much is too much? Is one call a day permissible?

Three a day? Once an hour? As a rule, if you greet your spouse saying, "Hi, it's me *again,*" you're calling too often. If you spend more time on hold with your spouse's workplace than you do with your children, it may be time to unplug the phone. If you sing along with the Muzak, you may need professional help.

A typical case of Spousal Call-itis:

9:03 A.M.

Housespouse: "Oh, good, you're there already. Do you know what Johnny did with his homework? No, I haven't looked under his bed. Why would it be under his bed? Hold on a second."

(Working Spouse casts longing look at coffee urn, where coworkers are gossiping.)

Housespouse: "You were right. It was under his bed. Go figure. Okay, have a great day. I'll talk to you later."(WS hangs up, fighting off sense of foreboding.)

10:27 A.M.

HS: "Hi, it's me again. Your mother called and ..."(WS tunes out, busy with incoming e-mail.)

HS (several minutes later): "So it's all right with you if I tell her we'll come over for dinner on Sunday?"

WS: "Yes."

HS: "Okay. I'll call her back. Hope the rest of your day goes well."

10:33 A.M.

HS: "Me again. Your mother now says Sunday's no good. How about Saturday?"

WS (balancing a teetering stack of paperwork that rivals most landfills): "Yes."

10:45 A.M.

HS: "I'm back. She now says Sunday would be better after all. I swear, I don't know what's wrong with that woman." (WS loses focus, busy making placating hand gestures to red-faced supervisor, who's pointing at wristwatch.)

1:02 P.M.

HS: "Oh, good, you're back from lunch. The refrigerator is making a funny noise."

WS (sighing heavily): "What kind of noise?"

HS: "Sort of whish-whish, then a clunk."

WS: "That's the icemaker."

HS: "Really? How come I've never noticed that before? I swear, I'm going goofy, working here all by myself. Listen, while I've got you on the phone . . ." (WS closes eyes and clenches jaw.)

2:17 P.M.

HS: "Me again. I was wondering, do we need new drapes in the living room? I've got a catalog here that has some that might do nicely . . ." (WS feels drops of blood popping out on forehead.)

3:23 P.M.

HS: "I know you're busy, but how about meat loaf for supper?"

WS: "Yes, yes, yes. Meat loaf would be wonderful. I've got to go now."

HS: "You want meat loaf with gravy or with that gooey ketchup all over the top?"

WS: "If I don't get back into that meeting, I'm going to be meat loaf myself."

HS (hurt): "Okay, sorry. Bye."

3:46 P.M.

WS: "Hi, it's me. Sorry I was abrupt before. But I was in this meeting and my boss—"

HS: "Hmph. If I'm bothering you at work, just say so. Am I calling too often?"

WS (seeing life flash before eyes): "Not at all, sweet-heart. I know it's important that we stay in touch throughout the day. You call whenever you want."

HS (somewhat mollified): "All right then. Only one more question for the busy, big-shot decision-maker. Mashed potatoes or fries?"

GOING IT ALONE:
WHEN MOM'S AWAY, THE HOUSEHOLD WILL DECAY

Okay, let's say you've learned to be No. 2 in the household, behind your fully employed wife. You can do it all—work, field trips, meals, cleaning, laundry, haircuts, doctor's appointments—without worrying her with the daily details of keeping the family together. You've got the work-at-home thing down.

Oh, yeah? Then let her go out of town for a week.

I've had this humbling experience, and I found that standards fall when no one is around to watch. The house becomes a pigsty. The kids wear holey jeans to school because Dad was too late and too exasperated to make them change. Phone calls go unreturned. Macaroni-and-cheese suddenly seems like a mighty fine supper. Competitive belching is acceptable after-dinner behavior.

Is it the same for wives who work at home? At my sons' school, I see the stay-at-home moms in their J. Crew ensembles and their Buddhist calm, and I wonder what it's like for them when Dad's out of town. Do things fall apart? Do they resort to giving their children spit-baths at red lights on the way to school? Do they dig deep into closets rather than do laundry, until they end up padding around the house in plaid shirts, jam-stained sweatpants, and crunchy socks? Does an inordinate amount of their time become devoted to computer games and ESPN? I think not.

But you send Mom out of town and even the most organized dad soon will be ready to check "all of the above."

Without women around to impress, we men quickly lose the battle against sloth. It's a lot of work, keeping up the house, cooking, and chauffeuring the kids, and there's almost always an easier alternative. Ignore the dirt (it'll still be there when I get around to it). Get drive-through fast-food (the clerks don't care whether I'm wearing shoes). Skip Cub Scouts this week (I can't let the other parents see me like this).

Slothful Dad falls into a television stupor while it all piles up. He's slugging beer and flipping channels, alternating between three different basketball games and *Baywatch*. Meanwhile, the unwashed kids are running around the house naked, eating cat food out of the can, and setting fire to the dog. It's *Lord of the Flies* in suburbia.

Heaven forbid that the whole family go out of town and leave Dad home alone. That's happened to me a few times, and the devolution is rapid and severe. Within hours of the family's departure, I've become a cave-dweller. All the window blinds are closed so that I get no glare on the TV. I'm wearing rags. I'm scratching myself without checking to see whether anyone watches. I'm burping at will. There's filth beneath my bare feet and a dog lying nearby, gnawing a bone. It's a wonder I don't start playing with fire and painting primitive hunting scenes on the walls.

It all comes to a halt, of course. No matter how much of a Neanderthal the man becomes, he knows that eventually he'll have to return to the present. Clean the house. Stock the cupboards. Bathe the children, the dog, himself. The fact that this all will occur in the last few hours before the wife's return is a given. What's the point of procrastination if you don't wait until the last possible minute? Then it's a frenzy, a whirlwind, a slam-bang race to the finish. Clean everything. Cook a meal. Pass out fresh clothes, bandages, and toothbrushes to the troops, along with a final debriefing on "Things we won't tell Mom."

And then Mom breezes in, flushed with happiness, and finds the place just as she left it. And she congratulates Dad on keeping everything so orderly. And Dad beams with pride, all the while wondering what's on ESPN.

A QUIZ:
ARE YOU KEEPING YOUR SPOUSE HAPPY?

We who do battle on the home front often get so busy with deadlines, child-care, and computer crashes that we neglect the care and feeding of the ones who make our stay-at-home lifestyle possible—our working spouses.

Our mates come home from a hard day at the office and we greet them with complaints and teeth-gnashing instead of caresses and kisses. We carp about overflowing toilets, Science Fair projects, stubborn children, and dog-chewed shoes.

This is not what the working partners need. The home may be our workplace, but to them it's sanctuary, a safe harbor after being tossed about the stormy seas of office politics and ringing phones. We homebodies need to make the house a warm, welcoming place so that our hard-working spouses will keep returning there after their long days of toil. Otherwise, they might dump us and we'll have to go out and get real jobs.

Here, then, is a self-scoring quiz aimed at making sure you're doing your best to keep your working spouse happy. There are no right answers, but perhaps these questions will make you stop and think whether you're doing your best for domestic bliss. Remember: the household income, health insurance, and that 401(k) may depend on whether you succeed.

> *Question:* After a hard day at the office, the thing your spouse needs most is:
> (A) warm greetings and a hot meal
> (B) a massage
> (C) a shot of bourbon
> (D) Valium

Question: When you meet your spouse at the door, you're wearing:

    (A) nice clothes and freshly brushed hair

    (B) sweatpants and three days' growth of whiskers

    (c) threadbare pajamas

    (D) Saran Wrap

Question: Your favorite pet name for your working spouse is:

    (A) darling

    (B) sweetheart

    (c) hey, stupid

    (D) sugar booger

Question: The first question out of your mouth when your spouse arrives home from work is:

    (A) "How was your day?"

    (B) "What's wrong?"

    (c) "Where have you been for the past three hours?"

    (D) "Is that lipstick on your collar?"

Question: When your spouse complains about his/her boss, you respond with:

    (A) "You poor thing!"

    (B) "Is there anything I can do to help?"

    (c) "You think you've got it bad? Today, I had to drive to two soccer practices. Then I had to call the plumber, and you know how much he charges. I don't know where we'll get the money. Then the dog . . ."

    (D) "Let's kill your boss."

Question: Working spouses are hungry when they get home. What kind of meal can your spouse expect?

    (A) roast venison with shallots and an expensive bottle of wine

(B) Chinese take-out
(C) TV dinners
(D) cold Spaghetti-O's

Question: The first sound your mate hears upon entering the house is:
   (A) "Welcome home, sweetheart!"
   (B) screaming children
   (C) weeping
   (D) repeated flushing

Question: Your children usually greet your spouse with:
   (A) hugs and kisses
   (B) a litany of the latest playground injuries
   (C) demands for money
   (D) derision

Question: On special occasions, your spouse can expect:
   (A) flowers delivered to the office
   (B) a babysitter and a night out on the town
   (C) a night out on the town *with* the babysitter
   (D) What's a special occasion?

Question: Most evenings, your mate can expect several hours of:
   (A) television
   (B) more work brought home from the office
   (C) complaining and bickering
   (D) sex

Question: Overall, the best thing you can give your working spouse is:
   (A) comforting words and a shoulder to cry on
   (B) a clean house and a hot meal
   (C) sex
   (D) a divorce

MAKING TIME
TO MAKE TIME

(A note: the following contains repeated references to sex, and you might want to keep it out of the reach of children and other non-believers. I don't want to offend any readers, so I've substituted *euphemisms* for certain words throughout. You who are in the know will understand. Wink, wink.)

Working parents have trouble finding time for *wrestling*. We're harried all day, surrounded by ringing telephones and other distractions. Evenings are filled with feeding, watering, and bedding down the herd. Somewhere in there, we must find time to *kvetch* about our workday and to listen to our spouses' tales of woe. By bedtime, we're too weary and frazzled to attempt any *noodling*, even though it's the most relaxing thing we could do and we'd probably sleep better.

Regular "alone time" is hard to come by in a household with children. But couples need that closeness, that recurrent *fiscal* contact, to make sure their relationship comes first. Couples who want to keep the whole household happy must make time to *tango*. In the harum-scarum of everyday life, you can forget to keep your *wok* life on the front burner. You can even lose the urge to *stir-fry*. One answer is to keep your *cuisine* interesting by being creative and imaginative—and even a little *kumquat*.

First, some basic advice for each gender:

WOMEN:

Nothing is more important to a man than his *fireplug*.

Men are visual creatures—we like to look—which is why self-help books recommend greeting your man at the door with your *poodle* wrapped in Saran Wrap.

Men are never too tired. We'll say we're too tired. We may not be in the mood at first. But we'll come around.

MEN:

Be gentle, especially when touching your mate's *petunias*.

Never, ever wrap any part of yourself in Saran Wrap, especially if you are the hairy sort.

Sometimes, women are not in the mood for *tomfoolery*. Live with it. This is why you must be ever-vigilant. Repeat after me: we men are never too tired. Who knows when you'll next get a moment with your wife? Strike while the *iron* is hot.

Now, let's talk about how you can be creative and keep the spark in your *ignition*. Spontaneity is important, so you'll need to plan ahead. Think of times when you and your spouse might be in the same room without children or dogs present. Think of ways you could turn these brief encounters into moments of passionate *combustion*. You can't always wait until bedtime. Everybody will be tired and *crankshaft* by then. Look for other times throughout the day when you can squeeze in a little *STP*.

One way to keep your *circumnavigation* exciting is to change your location. Try *galloping* on the sofa, on a desk, or in a steamy bathroom. Remember when you were a teen, and you did all your heavy *respirating* in the back seat of a car? Or how about that movie *Bull Durham*, where the characters *kneaded dough* right on the kitchen table? *Skewering* somewhere other than the same old bed might be just the thing to put the zing back in your *frisbee*.

Take turns being in charge. Sometimes the man makes the first move, sometimes the woman *initiates contact*. Urge your partner to *laminate* you, and eagerly take the lead when it's your turn to *play the kazoo*. Keep it playful, *swaggart*, and fun.

Experiment! Try different techniques and positions when you're *rewinding*. For example, if the man usually *jigsaws* on top, then you could try it with the woman in a *fully locked and upright position*. Try it with the man on his *cypresses* and the woman hanging her *feet* off the *transom*. For a quick rendezvous while the kids are watching TV, you can even *walk the dog* while leaning against the *light-pole* in the *loo*. The man can caress his partner's *tamales* while *introducing* his *stethoscope* to her *dust-buster*. Or the woman can *masticate* her man with gentle *turbulence* while *achieving altitude* herself by using her *howitzer* to *matriculate* an *organism*.

Whew.

So there's some sex advice for working couples. Was it good for you? It was over so quickly . . .

8.

SO YOU DON'T KNOW YOUR A:/DRIVE FROM A HOLE IN THE GROUND

Personal computers are marvelous inventions that make it possible for millions of people to work from home. They're also the biggest time-wasters ever created. In terms of hours lost, computers make television look like a good societal investment.

Like a lot of stay-at-home workers, I spend all day at the computer. It's my friend, my connection to the outside world, the electronic wonder that allows me to rewrite the same paragraph nine different ways without erasing. It's also my dreaded enemy, scheming to keep me from working, telling me my file isn't found, or "a fatal error has occurred."

With computers, the focus of the job often becomes the tool itself, not the end result. They often mean half the productivity in twice the time. And we entrust our work, investments, addresses, shopping, and record-keeping to machines that don't function when the power fails or when they get sick with a virus.

Add up all the time I spend sorting through files, tackling balky programs, and referring to "Help" and I might be better off writing with a quill pen. Even when the computer's working like the whiz-bang gizmo it's designed to be, it comes with built-in distractions. Tough sentence got me stumped? Time to check the e-mail. Don't know what comes next in my novel? I hear a computer game calling my name.

E-mail, like the computer itself, is a double-edged sword—one with blood on the blade. It's possible to do most of our business by e-mail these days, sending quick missives to coworkers or clients and keeping everyone abreast of our progress. It's also an incredible time sink.

We click into the Internet, just to make a quick check for urgent mail. Nothing important there, so we should click out again, get back to work. But wait. There's a message from a buddy, the latest bawdy joke making its way around the ether. Ha ha, that's a good one. So good, in fact, that we should share it with all our friends. Easy enough to do. Forward that puppy to everybody in the address book. Nice little day brightener. Of course, they, too, will waste time reading it and chuckling, but, hey, laughter is good for the soul. What's the point of everybody working at home if we can't take a moment to laugh?

Okay, now we can get back to work. But wait—there's another message. A reply from some other poor sap who's wasting his workday. Look, he liked the joke and he's sending one in return. That's only fair. Ha ha. Better forward that one, too. Ought to check the horoscope, too. Plus, the latest news, the chat groups, and the Usernet servers. Got to keep current. Next thing you know, it's dinner time.

Then there are the games. I upgraded to Windows after a decade with a machine that was a glorified typewriter. I swore I would not fall into the trap that had claimed so many of my friends. No Flight Simulator or Myst for me. Keep distractions to a minimum. The computer is a tool. I'm here to work. But Windows comes with solitaire built right in. Got to try it. They say it's good practice for learning proper control of your mouse. Once I'd worn out that deck, there was free gaming software beckoning on the Internet. Couldn't hurt to download a few. Be good for the kids to have more games. Get them comfortable with the computer. The more I played the games (including the ones for the kids), the more hooked I became. As soon as I mastered one game, I'd tackle a new one—anything to keep from actually working.

Before long, it was time to get on the virtual wagon.

ANOTHER NIGHT OF COFFEE
AND CARPING AT GAMERS ANONYMOUS

Hi, my name is Steve, and I'm a computer game junkie. (All together now: "Hi, Steve!")

I'm a little nervous. This my first time to come forward. I've been in denial a long time. But I was sitting in the back there, swilling coffee, and I thought: stand up and say it. Admit it to these strangers and maybe you can finally admit it to yourself. So that's what I'm doing. I'm confessing my sins. Who knows? Maybe it'll help.

My story is a familiar one. I started out small, just a little solitaire when no one was else was around. Maybe do a little shareware at parties. I told myself I was just experimenting. A taste of computer poker never hurt anybody, right? I still functioned in my everyday life, though sometimes I'd have a hangover the next morning from staying up too late, zapping aliens. Pretty soon, I was no longer just joy-popping. I moved up to the harder stuff— advanced games like Tetris that eat up your time and lead to debilitating physical problems, such as carpal tunnel syndrome.

My addiction started to crop up during the workday. I'd be itching to play when I should be doing something productive. I began to ignore my chores in favor of computer chess. I'd get irritated when the ringing phone interrupted a game that couldn't be paused. I skipped bathing, eating, and other everyday activities that might take me away from the computer screen. I'd bark at my children when they broke my concentration, pestering me with some minor problem, like a house fire. I was blind to all these signals, of course. I thought I had my habit under control.

I first recognized that I had a problem when I started attributing human motives to my computer, which is just a machine, after all. The computer seemed out to defeat me at any cost, and I began to treat it like a real, live, human enemy. I'd curse at it, pound the keyboard, choke the mouse, and generally act like an idiot.

Some of you are nodding. Guess you've been there, too, huh? But I went even further. I started believing the computer was toying with me.

Here's an example: one of my obsessions is a simple little game in which you fly around in a spaceship, shooting kamikaze aliens that are trying to crash into you. A silly game, really. It's called Evolve because the aliens change if you don't shoot them soon enough. They go from green to yellow to red with an increase in speed and agility in each incarnation. At first, I just played the game, win or lose, it didn't matter. But then I began to notice a pattern. Just when I'd killed nearly all the aliens and was relaxing a bit, bracing to move up to the next level, one of the few remaining aliens would evolve suddenly and run right at my ship at twice the normal speed. How else to explain it? The evil computer was out to get me.

Another game involves moving virtual marbles around a board. I started to believe the computer was counting ahead two or three plays, so it could be sure to trap me. It took all the joy out of the game. Now, I get so caught up in trying to read the machine's motives that, *boom*, I lose all my marbles.

It's insanity to play a counting game against a computer, anyway; counting is what they do best. But I keep playing. I'm hooked. And now I've admitted it. I'm planning to get with the program and kick the habit.

Withdrawal will be rough. My hands will itch to play again. My brain will desire the strategy, the competition, the occasional victory. I'll hear the beeping and blooping of the games in my sleep. But I think I'm ready. I just hope it's not too late.

I know you're supposed to stop cold turkey, but I was wondering, could I do just a little more Tetris before I get on the wagon? I'm ready to quit. Really. But first I want to teach that computer a lesson.

NO LONGER AM I
A MAN OF LETTERS

Draft of a letter to be sent to dozens of people I used to know:

"Dear friend:

"I know it's been a long time since you've heard from me. I regret that I've been so remiss in my correspondence. Sure, we've talked on the phone, but it's been months. Remember how we once wrote letters every week or two? We kept in touch, made sure the old friendship stayed intact.

"I could make excuses for not writing to you sooner. I could say I work as a writer, I use up all my words in my prose, and all my time being creative. But that would be a lie. I'm never at a shortage of words. And I spend much valuable time playing cards with my computer.

"I could blame the computer itself. It has seduced me. Every free moment is given over to that accursed machine. It has made me a wastrel and a loner.

"I could blame my children. The little ragamuffins devour all my free time, leaving me harried and distracted. By the time I've fed them, clothed them, and bossed them through a long day of chores and bickering, I'm too exhausted to compose a letter to an old friend.

"I could blame what passes for coworkers in this lonely life of a work-at-home dad. My agent, my editors, and my colleagues all make demands upon me, demands I often am unworthy to meet. I therefore spend much of my time faking it, which keeps me too busy to properly answer my correspondence.

"But, in fact, dear friend, I blame you. See, you still don't have e-mail. I frankly don't understand how you function in the modern world without it, but I guess that is a choice you've made and I shouldn't question it. Lots of you low-tech Luddites manage to lead productive lives, I'm sure.

"E-mail has spoiled me. I can fire off missives to the

electronic 'haves' among my friends in minutes, sending the latest news, snort of humor, or just a quick hello without bothering with the formalities of paper and envelopes. My correspondents can reply just as quickly, so that sometimes we write back and forth several times in a single day. No waiting by the mailbox in this modern world. Just a quick check of the electronic mail, oh, seven or eight times a day, as easy as clicking a few keys and waiting for that warm, familiar voice to say, 'You have mail.'

"No addresses to remember, no zip codes to hunt up. Just click on a button and spew your reaction directly onto the screen. We often don't even bother with salutations or greetings of any kind. The computer tells the recipient who sent the mail and that's enough information for such rapid, informal correspondence. I even find myself forgetting to use capital letters and punctuation. E-mail is more like a quick chat than a formal conversation. Dash off a few words, hit the 'send' button and move on to the next.

"Real letters, printed on paper, seem so permanent that they require more care. There are all those rules about addresses and spacing. So many choices to be made: 'Best wishes' versus 'Yours truly' or 'Sincerely yours.' What if the recipient saves the letter and shows it to others? Better not have any typos, incoherent passages, or risqué jokes in there for all the world to see. All those things are allowed—even encouraged—in e-mail.

"And once I've struggled through composing such a letter, making sure every 'i' is dotted and every sentence succinct, there's the act of mailing it. Scrounging around in search of postage stamps, which seem so old-fashioned and expensive. Better to pay thirty bucks a month to America Online than to be nibbled at, thirty-seven cents at a time.

"So, dear friend, this will be the last letter you receive from me. It's all just too much effort and expense. But let me know when you get e-mail. Then we'll be in touch again.

"Sincerely yours,

"Steve Brewer"

COMPUTERS DON'T SAVE PAPER,
IT'S ALL AT MY HOUSE

Whatever happened to the "paperless office?" Remember those predictions, how the computer would eliminate paper from our lives? Everything would be handled electronically. No need for millions of trees to surrender their lives so we can pulp them into clean white sheets that we clutter up with ink.

Those forecasts went into the same trash heap as the predictions that we'd all be flying around in hovercars by now and spending our weekends on Mars. We use more paper than ever. Paper gives us a permanent record, something to file away, safe from the hazards of hard-drive crashes and unwise decisions to "delete."

(I've always thought the "delete" button should be labeled "oops." Same with the "escape" key. Hell, the way I type some days, they all could be labeled "oops.")

For at-home workers, the paper piles up until it threatens to bury everything in the household. We don't have secretaries or file clerks to take it away and stash it somewhere, never to be seen again. We do our own filing, if any, and it can be as haphazard as the rest of our disorganized lives.

The answer, I'm sure, is to embrace the technology and stop generating so much paper. Store everything in the computer, back up every file, and keep a log of file names and document folders. But that's all too methodical for a guy who can barely organize a sock drawer.

Even if I wanted to reduce the paper flow from my life, my work wouldn't allow it. Book publishers still do most everything on paper. Manuscripts are passed around publishing houses from editor to editor like batons in a slow-motion relay race. Here's how high-tech they get in the book industry: each editor uses a different color ink to mark corrections, leaving a trail of who-did-what. Take that, Bill Gates.

I do the same thing at home. I print a manuscript, mark it up with a lot of changes, then transfer the changes to the computer copy. Then I print out a new version and start the process all over again. By the time I'm finished, I could stack manuscripts to the ceiling.

Generating all those documents means using the "print" command. That key should be labeled "commit to paper now, only to discover typographical errors once it's printed and then do it all over again." But I guess that wouldn't fit on the keyboard.

Back when we used typewriters, everyone was accustomed to penciled-in changes and flaky blurs of correcting fluid. But now that computers are ubiquitous, we all expect perfect copy. And that means printing and fixing and reprinting and fixing, ad infinitum.

For years, I was stuck using a slow, dot-matrix printer. Each line of type required a moving head to needle the words onto the paper. Apparently, it was a painful process because the printer made a high-pitched wail with every line. I called it "The Screamer." Printing out a three-hundred-page manuscript would leave my ears ringing for days.

I now use a faster, quieter laser printer. It's wonderful until something goes wrong with it. Then I'm reminded how we at-home workers are trapped alone with our problems. In a regular office, you call the technical types and they wheel the balky printer away and bring it back when it's repaired. At home, you're on your own.

Recently, I was rushing through a print job when a gray stripe started appearing down the middle of each page. I discovered this problem, naturally, after fifty or so striped pages were on their way to the wastebasket. I opened the printer and cleaned it out. I thumbed through the user's manual. I finally hurried to an office supplies store and bought a new toner cartridge, to the tune of sixty-five dollars. All was well again. Except all my monkeying with the printer's innards meant that the paper no longer fed smoothly. A page would go halfway into the machine, then the printer would emit a groaning noise and everything would lock up. Then I would emit a groaning noise and start all over again.

So "The Screamer" has been replaced by "The Groaner." Quill pens, anyone?

RAISE A STINK WITH YOUR E-MAIL

In the pantheon of Bad Applications of New Technologies, here's one that really stinks: several companies reportedly are perfecting ways to transmit aromas over your e-mail. That's right, folks— smell-mail. Just when you thought the Internet couldn't possibly get any more intrusive, they've found a way to download odors.

The technology varies from company to company, but essentially it works like this: you'd have a device hooked to your computer that would contain an array of aromatic chemicals. When someone e-mailed you a picture of, say, a strawberry, you would slide a piece of adhesive paper through the device. The paper would pick up the appropriate chemicals and, once spit out by the machine, the paper would carry the scent of a strawberry.

Other companies are working on versions that would mix chemicals stored on a cartridge and actually waft the aroma into your room with a small fan. So it isn't exactly like transmitting actual odors over the Internet. It's more like a digitized simulation. But it's still an exceedingly bad idea.

We all know these things tend to get out of hand. Already, people e-mail goofy, animated greeting cards for every holiday. Websites have soundtracks of obnoxious music. Every time you visit a site, your computer is fed "cookies" that result in a deluge of advertising spam. Now, we're going to make it possible for people to send their favorite aromas along, too?

Virtual flower bouquets undoubtedly will be among the first uses. That annual holiday letter—already a pain because you're forced to read how some distant relative is doing much better than you—could include the evergreen scent of the family Christmas tree.

It's bad enough that chirpy friends can send you a cute photo of the family dog. What happens when they can send along his smell, too? That's what you need: Essence de Wet Dog spilling out into your house. If you wanted that smell around, you could hose down your own dog and save the hundreds of dollars the digital scent generators cost.

The developers of these new devices say the applications are endless. You could have smells accompanying your favorite movies, they say. Or you could sample a perfume before purchasing it over the Internet. Cookie and candy companies have expressed interest in using the technology for samples. (There goes the diet.) They're even perfecting a "new car" smell to accompany auto ads.

This technology could easily fall into the wrong hands. If your friends send you sweet little fragrances and your computer smells like fresh-baked cookies, how long before one of your enemies gets hold of your smell-mail address? Pretty soon, you've got the stink of sweaty socks filling your home office. I don't even want to think what the purveyors of Internet porn might do with this.

Won't hackers have a field day, too? They've been able for years to send viruses, worms, and other terroristic programs to computers all over the globe. What happens when they decide the virtual world needs a sniff of stockyard stench? Or, when they decide to protest government policies by sending federal offices a fetid whiff of body odor?

Worse yet, some of the same companies that are working up virtual aromas also are working on taste transmittal. That strawberry mentioned earlier? You can lick the paper and taste the berry, or a chemical facsimile. Do we need this? Couldn't we just stop at a supermarket and buy actual strawberries?

Already, many of the e-mails we receive every day are in bad taste (particularly jokes sent by friends—you know who you are). What happens when actual bad tastes can arrive unbidden over your computer? Are you willing to take a chance on licking a piece of paper that purports to be chocolate? Could be garlic or broccoli—or worse.

Not me, buddy. The day that virtual food and fragrances start arriving on my computer is the day I dust off the typewriter. The scent of correction fluid I can handle. The rest you can keep to yourself.

BLIND ANONYMITY
LEADS TO SLINGS AND ARROWS

I called a man a "twit" recently. This isn't like me. Don't get me wrong, I can be as guilty of name-calling as the next purported grown-up. But, like most people, I prefer to spread my slurs in the safe zone behind the other man's back. If I get riled enough to go face-to-face with somebody, we've usually moved beyond the "twit" stage and into the shouting of unprintables.

But this wasn't a face-off. It was via e-mail. And this guy had said something so, so *twittish* that somebody had to call him on it.

The occasion arose on a mailing list called DorothyL, which is for readers and writers of mysteries. Delivered daily by e-mail, the list resembles an extended conversation about books among nearly three-thousand members.

One member was facing a serious illness, and asked others to send her messages that said they were burning candles for her. She was making a map with these "points of light" all over the globe as an inspiration to get well. Hundreds of us replied; it was going sweetly until one snarky guy complained that the messages had nothing to do with the topic of the list—mystery stories.

Now, I don't know this guy. I don't know the ailing woman, either. So why did his message enrage me so? Within seconds, I was boiling. Within minutes, the message had been sent. *Zoom*, with all the speed of e-mail. Delivered to the list for all to see. Twit.

As is typical of these virtual conversations, a flame war quickly ignited. Some defended the twit. Others pounced on him, as I had. After two days of bickering, the manager of the list ordered everybody to cool it. Within a week, the list was in an uproar over some other slight, and I cackled loudly while watching the battle from the safety of my home office. This time, I stayed out of it.

For those of us who work at home, such virtual neighborhoods can become too familiar. There are mailing lists and newsgroups out there on the Internet for every interest—everything from sheepdogs to Sherlock Holmes. What begins as a font of information soon becomes a source of camaraderie. We develop virtual friendships. And, like kids on a playground choosing up sides, we make virtual enemies, too. Before you know it, you're calling somebody a twit. Or somebody's saying the same about you.

Because it's all said via e-mail, it carries the protection of anonymity and distance. Sure, you might attach your name to the flame, but there's no danger that the guy you call a twit is going to take a poke at you. The worst that can happen is someone who's wittier or meaner will get you back, that you'll become the butt of the joke or the target of the attacks. It may sting, but it's only e-mail, right? That's why computers come with a "delete" key.

The intriguing part is how something so remote becomes so emotional. I sometimes laugh aloud at others' postings. I was near to tears when a distraught DorothyL member reported the death of a well-loved author. And I clearly can be moved to anger by the occasional twitticism.

None of it is real. We're all alone, all of us, sitting at our computers, playing at friendship, enmity, and debate. Yet, it feels like a cocktail party, clamorous with gossip, argument, and inane chatter.

When pollsters ask telecommuters what they miss most about not going to a regular office, the answer usually has nothing to do with the work itself. Thanks to computers, modems, and the Internet, most of us can do our work anywhere. What we miss is the office environment: the internal politics, the hearsay, and the lunchtime conversations. We miss the watercooler.

And now the computer supplies that, too.

9.

Rearing Children, or Beware, Here Lie Monsters

One reason that many Americans choose to work at home is we can spend quantity time with our children. We heed the warnings from child-rearing experts who tell us it's important that one parent stay home so the children grow up somewhat normal and our property values remain intact.

But stay-at-home parents quickly learn that work and kids don't mix. Keeping children safe and amused is a full-time job all by itself (which is why so many couples pay someone else to do it). Try to earn some money while the kids are around and you'll end up with juice in the fax machine and peanut butter on your paperwork. Your chair will be surrounded by little piles of hair that you've pulled from your own head.

We love our children, but we also love our routines. We have deadlines to meet, phone calls to make, laundry piling up, coffee to drink, newspapers to read, and, my God, why can't we get a quiet moment around here?

I try to plan my work schedule so I'm essentially free when my two sons are not in school. I try to make days off just for them. Give them my full attention. Play with them, drive them places, and referee those caterwauling matches that always result from too much togetherness. But my best-laid plans invariably are scrambled by a last-minute phone call or e-mail, and I'm stuck trying to get some work done while the boys chase around the house, yelling and threatening and babbling and laughing.

I explain to them that I need to do a little work before our day of fun and adventure begins. I send them to the far end of the house to play, read, or watch TV, anything they want as long as it's not loud and distracting. They nod understandingly, then gallop several laps through the house, being loud and distracting. I run through the explanation again; they express their apologies before hurrying away to mix up a baking-soda-and-vinegar "volcano." I stop what I'm doing and clean up that mess. I then state firmly that they simply must go do something quiet and non-destructive—outdoors—while I work. They promise to do their best and scurry away, heads down, trying to remember where they hid the matches.

By the time my wife comes home from work, I'm a wreck. The work may or may not have been accomplished. The kids are cowed and irritable and sick of being home with blustery old Dad, who never lets them do anything fun.

Kids don't come equipped with "off" buttons. And it's not just my kids. I recently spent an entire Saturday in the company of boys. First, I hosted a small birthday party for my younger son. Then we hustled around and got into uniform and attended a banquet for Cub Scouts and their parents. I don't know exactly how many Scouts attended the meeting, but a conservative estimate would be eight gazillion. And they were all squirming, whooping, running, picking their noses, and smearing cake on each other, just like my boys. I sat quietly, in a sleep-deprived stupor, trying to remember what I was working on the last time the boys let me have a turn at the computer.

How do teachers do it all day, five days a week, during the school year? I can barely keep two kids sane and unbloodied when we're together all day. What if I had to face twenty or thirty howling children? Teachers are the best example of Your Tax Dollars at Work.

And what about those parents who have preschool children? They should plan to get their work done sometime in the future.

Say, when their kids reach graduate school. Actually, I have a comforting message for those of you who have children under the age of six: it gets easier.

As children get older, parents move from the trenches to the rear guard, in charge of logistics rather than patrolling the sleepless front lines of the home front. So it's like a promotion, and, in many ways, there's less incoming flak.

When they're toddlers, kids seem to be in constant danger—teetering on stacked boxes to reach stuff, experimenting with matches and electrical sockets, teething on the dog. With experience, children learn which things to put in their mouths and where not to stick their fingers. They discover that you'll reach high shelves for them if they whine enough. Once children learn to solve their own problems, parents can relax a little. They can get a full night's sleep occasionally. Most important, parents can bend over a lot less, which becomes crucial with age.

A case in point: my wife bought these bean-bag chairs so our two sons could drag them around and flop into them in front of various television sets strategically placed around the house. The bean bags look like big old prunes lying on the floor, and you can trip over them in the dark, but they keep the kids off the good furniture, which is important, particularly when they're noshing Pringles.

One bean bag sprang a leak—thanks to the dog—and my nine-year-old recognized the leak as a problem he could solve. He went to the junk drawer in the kitchen and got out scissors and duct tape (that's my boy!). He crouched over the bean bag, cut tape to the right length with the scissors and—voila!—the repair was made. And he didn't approach me for help. How did I even know he'd accomplished this on his own? Well, the junk drawer was hanging open, for one thing. Duct tape and scissors sat out on the counter. He hadn't put anything away when he was done. If this seems like shoddy workmanship to you, then you're missing the point. He'd done part of the job himself. And it was the part that involved bending over.

When I was a kid growing up in the South, my parents considered my brother and me to be their own personal remote controls. We could be out in the yard playing, and they'd call us inside to change the channel or fetch more tea. My parents believed it was easier to shout a kid down from upstairs than to get up and cross the room and turn on a lamp.

From a tender age, I hated this. I didn't see why I needed to interrupt my important activities—which usually centered on slaying imaginary Nazis—just because a parent didn't want to dislodge from the La-Z-Boy.

Now that I'm a middle-aged parent of two strapping boys, I do the same thing. I'm General Dad. I sit in my comfy chair, a newspaper spread across my lap, my coffee within arm's reach, and I invariably spy something that needs doing. Time to summon the troops. Yo, boys! Come here and hand me that/pick that up/clean that up/put that down/turn that off. They mutter and drag their feet, but they do it. And I don't have to wrestle my way up out of my chair.

I see now why my parents used my brother and me as their servants. Parents are tired all the time. We never really catch up on our rest from those 2 A.M. feedings. And bending over and picking things up off the floor becomes increasingly difficult for aging spines. Better to let the kids do it. They need the exercise. They're limber. They're closer to the floor.

I know this won't last. Before long, my boys will be teenagers, and I'll be lucky if I can find them, much less get them to help me. And shouting the length of the house for assistance does no good when the kids always wear headphones spewing rap music. But until then, I've got helpers, my own little chain gang. Now all I need is a La-Z-Boy.

WHEN THE KIDS ARE HOME, PART I: WEEKENDS

At a recent backyard birthday party, the entertainment was a menagerie of snakes and other creatures the kids could handle. The kids were on Cloud Nine. I fidgeted a lot, guzzling beer and trying to hide my discomfort. To me, a snake in the yard means go get the hoe.

In the midst of this merriment, a beaming, stay-at-home mom turned to me and said, "Don't you miss them now that they're back in school?"

"Who, the kids?" I replied, taking it as a joke. "Hahahahaha."

"No, really," she said. "I get lonely at home all day."

That was enough to make me forget the snakes for a while.

Lonely? At home? With the kids in school where they belong? It never even occurs to me. In fact, I have just the opposite problem. I get testy on weekends when everyone's home. So much noise and confusion, so much anxiety and conflict resolution and food preparation. I secretly look forward to Monday morning, when the place becomes all mine again.

It doesn't help that my sons try to pack a week's worth of adventures and mayhem into Saturday and Sunday. I spend an inordinate amount of time on weekends sprawled in my comfy chair in front of televised sports, the sound down low so I can hear what the boys are up to. Occasionally, I'll shout, "No!" and they'll abandon their latest feat of derring-do in favor of something less likely to result in stitches or broken teeth.

A case in point: the other day, the boys were playing with our crocodilian dog in the next room and I hear one tell the other, "Stick your hand in his mouth." No!

The day before: I'm walking past a kid's bedroom and hear this, "Let's make a springboard!" I stick my head through the door and say calmly, "No way. And put those mattresses back on the bunk beds."

Then there was this: I was sitting in my comfy chair, minding my own business, and trying to ignore the noisy frolicking in the next room. My older son bounces into the room where I'm hiding and hurls a paper airplane at me. It hits me squarely between the eyes.

Come on, you say, it was just a paper airplane. Couldn't have hurt much. True, but I wasn't even looking when it zoomed my way. The surprise was worse than the contact. For an instant, it was like getting beaned by a fastball. I nearly had a heart attack.

Nothing like this happens when I'm home alone. I almost never fall out of trees, walk on fences, or swat at power lines with broom handles. It's pretty easy to keep an eye on myself.

Aside from the chaos, there's also the housework problem. All week, I keep the house reasonably presentable because I'm home alone. I breeze around, putting away laundry, picking up toys, and occasionally doing something really strenuous like sweeping. Every night, the kids do their best to undo that work, but they only have a few hours between school and bedtime, and they can't wreck the place entirely.

But on weekends, they've got all day to strew, scatter, and soil. Snack-wrappers, dirty socks, baseball cards, crayons, and comic books materialize everywhere. I follow the boys around, policing the area, but always end up retreating to my comfy chair. There's no keeping up with them; it's two against one. But I surrender with the knowledge that I'll live to clean again, even if it takes until Wednesday to recover from the weekend.

And I can recover in blissful solitude, a lone creature tending his den, quietly surviving, hidden away from the hustle-bustle of the outside world. Hmm. Kind of like a snake.

WHEN THE KIDS ARE HOME, PART II: SUMMERS

Ah, summer vacation. Lazy afternoons at the swimming pool. Cookouts and camping trips. Cries of "Dad-deee! I'm bored! And make him stop *looking* at me!"

Summer is the time when work-at-home parents add "camp counselor" to their other job titles—maid, cook, handyman, lawn boy, chauffeur, laundry slave.

Each spring, the newspapers run whole sections listing summer camps, sports events, and other activities available to kids. These programs are educational, entertaining, and often expensive. Rather than spend money on camp, the thinking goes, shouldn't the work-at-home parent provide the summer amusements for the children? After all, it's three months of quality time, right? You can keep the kids at home, keep them busy, teach them something, and have fun together.

Smart parents make lists of possibilities ahead of time—museum outings, hiking excursions, road trips, and play dates. Then they use all those up in the first three weeks. What to do then? The summer yawns before you, day after idle day, interrupted only by spats and demands. You can only rent so many videos before the dazed little buggers get square eyes.

Here are some activities that can make your summer a happy, productive time with your kids. (Note: I take no responsibility for the results, particularly if social workers or lawyers become involved.)

SCAVENGER HUNTS

Children love to find things, which is how Easter egg hunts became a tradition. With just a little encouragement, they can entertain themselves for hours, searching the nooks and crannies of the house and yard for items you've hidden or lost. This is a wonderful way to keep the kids busy while finding those missing socks. Make it clear, however, that only parents are supposed to do the hiding. Otherwise, you'll never see your car keys again.

WATER PLAY

Slather them with sunscreen, turn on the hose, and hurry back into the house. They'll take it from there. Refuse to let them back inside until they're dry.

MUSICAL ACTIVITIES

An empty coffee can makes a pretty good drum. Whistles and kazoos are easily mastered. All you need is a set of earplugs, and you're in for a fun-filled afternoon. If your neighbors are home during the day, you might want to offer them earplugs, too.

CARD GAMES

Cards teach math and matching skills to children and can prove to be valuable social tools for their futures. A child shouldn't be expected to attend college, for instance, without a wholesome knowledge of poker. Not unless you want all the tuition money to go to some dorm shark named Morty. A child is never too young to learn that you don't draw to an inside straight. Card games are particularly good for those afternoons when it's too rainy to go outside and play. And strip poker can help kids cool off when it's too hot. Loser has to take a bath.

MAGIC TRICKS

This is another good indoor activity, though we should caution that the parent will be required to watch whatever little magic show the kids put together. Sounds like fun, but you try listening to "pick a card, any card" three dozen times. A length of sturdy rope can keep your burgeoning escape artist out of trouble for hours.

WEEDING

You can clean up that lawn and keep the children busy at the same time. Arm each child with a bucket and a blunt hand shovel, then tell them you'll pay a penny for every weed they dig up. This activity can end up running into some money, but it's still cheaper than an afternoon at Discovery Zone. Warning: not recommended for those who value their flowers and gardens. Children think everything is a weed, including grass. But then you can offer them a penny for every divot they replace.

After a while, they'll forget what they're supposed to be doing and end up playing outside, which was what you were trying to accomplish in the first place.

SCHOOL MORNINGS: QUICK! TO THE BAT-POLE

For parents, every school-day morning presents a mad dash to the bell. We scramble around the house like Keystone Kops in bathrobes, frenetically trying to get everyone fed, hosed off, dressed, brushed, backpacked, and out the door on time.

Here's how it goes at our house:

7 A.M.   Mom cheerfully awakens sleepy sons, then departs for work.

7:02 A.M.   Dad walks length of the house to kitchen, where he sets out bowls, spoons, napkins, cereal, and milk.

7:06 A.M.   Dad returns to bedroom, cheerfully reminds boys they should be in a fully locked and upright position.

7:08 A.M.   Dad, back in kitchen, pours himself more coffee. Starts singing, in a loud *Oklahoma* basso profundo, "I'm gonna be the first one ready. Oh, yes *I am.*"

7:11 A.M.   Dad returns to bedroom, finds boys have not risen to bait. Not so cheerfully reminds them that breakfast awaits.

7:15 A.M.   Dad lets dog outside for fourth time since arising. Sings some more.

7:20 A.M.   Dad rushes into bedroom, tickles boys until they either must get up or wet their pants.

7:22 A.M.   Boys run squealing to bathroom.

7:23 A.M.   Dad sends boys to kitchen. Reminds them departure is scheduled for 8:30 A.M.

7:25 A.M.   Dad steps on scale in his bathroom. Mutters curses. Shaves, showers, and stares into mirror remembering lost youth, locates and puts on clean clothes, checks teeth again, takes deep breath, and goes in search of sons.

8:06 A.M.   Finds them still in pajamas at kitchen table, flicking Froot Loops at each other.

8:07 A.M.   Dad suffers minor cardiac arrhythmia. Urges boys to jump into their clothes.

8:08 A.M.	Everyone sprints in different directions.
8:11 A.M.	Dad pours more coffee, notices hand is shaking.
8:12 A.M.	Dad races around, barking orders at boys, who blissfully ignore him.
8:15 A.M.	Older son, half-dressed, announces he forgot to do homework the night before. Dad melts into steaming puddle on floor.
8:19 A.M.	Having gotten older son seated in front of empty homework page, Dad hurries to other end of house, where he finds nine-year-old making motorboat noises with his mouth. Dad: "Why do you have a rocket ship in your hand instead of a sock?"
8:20 A.M.	Dad, back at table, sees older son has made progress on homework, though it's all unreadable. Dad suggests corrective measures.
8:24 A.M.	Dad returns to younger son's room, is informed son's shoes have been stolen.
8:25 A.M.	Frantic shoe hunt commences.
8:26 A.M.	Older son finishes homework, leaves it on dining table. Runs off to play.
8:27 A.M.	Frantic shoe hunt continues. Dad muttering, "I always know where *my* shoes are. How can a person lose his *shoes!*"
8:28 A.M.	Dad shouts for older son to join hunt. Older son can't be located.
8:29 A.M.	Shoes found under parents' bed. Younger son denies allegations he's been jumping on bed again.
8:30 A.M.	Dad screams commands. Sons wriggle into sweatshirts. Run off to bathroom to redo mussed hair.
8:31 A.M.	Dad grinds teeth.
8:32 A.M.	All three sprint to automobile like a pit crew.
8:33 A.M.	Dad discovers windshield is covered in frost.

	A frenzy of scraping ensues. Older son ambles back to house to get homework.
8:35 A.M.	Dad proceeds to school, zooming through traffic like Al Unser.
8:45 A.M.	Screeches to halt outside school.
8:46 A.M.	Boys choose this moment to ask important questions about life. Dad answers calmly, craving cigarette.
8:51 A.M.	Dad asks boys to eject from car, but they insist on hearing the end of Spin Doctors' song on the radio.
8:54 A.M.	Dad pushes boys out of car, bids them farewell with a fond, "Stay out of trouble today!"
8:55 A.M.	Bell rings.
9:07 A.M.	Dad arrives homes, exhausted and jittery. Finds that friendly elves have not cleaned kitchen in his absence. Kitchen looks like the dining room on the *Titanic*.
9:08 A.M.	Dad sighs wearily and begins cleaning.
9:18 A.M.	Dad finishes scraping barnacles off tabletop, pours more coffee, and settles into comfy chair at his desk. Turns on computer.
9:25 A.M.	After the usual two reboots, Dad is ready for workday to begin.

HELLO, 911?
WE'VE GOT AN OWIE HERE

It has come to our attention that you, the unwashed public, know as much about first aid as your average honeydew. You may feel confident that you could handle any emergency, but how much do you really know? For example, could you adequately perform STP or the Heineken Maneuver if a loved one's life was in danger?

Of course you couldn't. You'd be crying and running around

like the proverbial headless fowl. Serious emergencies are nothing to fool around with, and they're the reason we put up with telemarketers calling us seventeen times a day. For real emergencies, we have phones. We dial 911 and professional, live-saving types come running.

No, first aid is not for amateurs. But then, most household emergencies don't require a professional. Most fall into the category of (and we don't want to get too technical here) "Owies."

Parents by necessity become household doctors, performing triage on burns, bites, scrapes, and bruises several times a day. By the time our children are grown, we have spent as much time taking temperatures as your average veterinarian.

It takes a while for parents to learn how to make the treatment age-appropriate. When ministering to scrapes and other minor wounds, emotional comfort is as important as pain relief. Some parents overdo it. Others, especially those with older children, need actual pools of blood to make them get up off the couch.

What parents need are standardized triage procedures, so they'll know how to react when faced with minor injuries among children of all ages. We propose the following.

FOR CHILDREN UNDER AGE 3

STEP 1. Parent should panic.

STEP 2. Run around crazily.

STEP 3. Take deep breaths and get a grip on yourself. Child will be screaming until red in face, so don't try to quiet him yet. Steel yourself and examine wound.

STEP 4. Feel faint.

STEP 5. More deep breaths. Tell anyone who'll listen, "It'll be all right. It'll be all right."

STEP 6. Get out handy first-aid kit. Carefully clean wound while child howls. Apply the following: spray-on sunburn reliever, antiseptic, petroleum jelly, mercurochrome, iodine, aloe vera, ginseng, diaper cream, and various ointments.

STEP 7. Bandage wound.

mean the usual obstacle course of abandoned toys on the floor and cups of juice left sitting on antique tables. These are traps creatively designed just for me.

My ten-year-old rigs his bedroom door. He takes a half-deflated kickball and balances it on his nearly closed door. (Don't ask me how he reaches up there. I try not to think about it. For all I know, he's standing on his brother's shoulders like some circus act.) I step through the door and—*bomp!*—the ball hits me in the head. No harm done. Doesn't hurt. Gives the boys a good belly-laugh. But it surprises the heck out of me. Every time.

I try to ignore such tomfoolery, to keep my parental demeanor intact, but sometimes I fly off the handle, squawking at the kids to stop scaring me like that. This, of course, is what they were after.

One day, I was hurrying off someplace and I was dressed up (read: Dockers and a shirt with actual buttons) when my ten-year-old solemnly told me the kitchen sink was malfunctioning. I huffed exasperatedly and asked for details, thinking all the while: this is what I need. Yet another plumbing disaster when I'm already late.

"Come see," he said. I followed him to the kitchen, my suspicions growing.

"Turn it on," he said.

"What's it going to do?" I asked skeptically.

"Turn it on. You'll see."

I gingerly grasped the tap and turned it—and was immediately soaked. I shrieked, jumped up in the air, shut off the tap, and whirled in place.

The cold water was even more shocking because it hadn't come out of the faucet. It came from the spray hose set into the sink, the one we use to rinse off dishes.

Then I spotted the tape. Clear packing tape had been used to tape the squirter nozzle in the "fire" position. And the sprayer had been carefully aimed so it would water whoever turned on the faucet. In my case, it hit me in the stomach, soaking my shirt with actual buttons and the T-shirt underneath. Now I was really late for my appointment. And I had to change clothes.

The ten-year-old rolled on the floor, *har-harring*. I stood over him, dripping and shouting. After a minute or so, he realized I was really mad and sobered up enough to tell me his brother was the one who'd set the trap. Younger brother was just the shill, and he had no compunction about ratting out the real miscreant. I muttered about conspiracies, threatened punishments, and generally acted a fool. Then I went off to find a dry shirt (with buttons).

Incidents like these make me jumpy. I walk on eggshells all the time, vigilant for the next prank, ears cocked for the creak of floorboards or the anticipatory giggle. And, on those rare occasions when I catch them first, I wheel around and shout, *"Boo!"*

Serves 'em right.

IT'S SPOOKY HERE, EVEN WHEN THE KIDS AREN'T AROUND

My desk was "Grown in Washington State." The washing machine is a "Producto de Ecuador." And the kitchen counters are really "California Navels." This, at least, is what it says on the little stickers affixed to them.

You know which stickers I mean. The ones originally attached to fresh fruit. These stickers migrate throughout the house, fastening themselves onto every surface. I asked my sons how this keeps happening, and they are in agreement: "We don't know."

It's a mystery, one of those unexplained phenomena that occur all the time in homes where there are children. It's enough to make parents think their houses are haunted. Lights left on in unoccupied rooms. Radios turned on by unseen hands. Toys arranged on tabletops in arcane patterns, as if to spell out some message from the Great Beyond. Furniture moves around the room so I can find it in the dark with my little toe. Sometimes, whole rooms are rearranged into scenes from Dali paintings.

The most obvious deduction: the children are responsible for these eerie anomalies. But they deny all knowledge of how candy-wrappers end up in dresser drawers or how magazines get all wet. When confronted with such household conundrums, they go wide-eyed and shruggy. It's beyond explanation, they indicate, one of the universe's sly tricks.

If the boys are eliminated as suspects, that only leaves poltergeists. My wife certainly wouldn't go around putting fruit stickers on the furniture. And the dog doesn't have any fingers. He couldn't peel a sticker off an apple if his life depended on it.

Why would ghosts ply such mischief? If they want us out of the house, if we're sitting atop an ancient graveyard or something, they could give me one healthy "*Boo!*" and I'd sign over the deed in a flash. I saw *The Amityville Horror*. I wouldn't wait around until things got out of hand. But no, these ghosts' evil plot doesn't revolve around fright. They seem bent on annoying me until I falsely accuse my poor innocent children of leaving puddles of sticky juice on the floor.

These apparitions apparently are computer-literate. Every time I sit down at my computer, all the settings have been changed. Unfamiliar wallpaper greets me. Icons are rearranged on the desktop. The ghosts leave disks or CD-ROMs in drives, which confuses an awakening computer, forcing reboots. Phantom files appear that can be neither opened nor deleted. My cursor, normally a quick one-dimensional arrow, becomes a staggering drunk of a pointer, leaving little images of itself in its wake.

Grave annoyances, but my children swear they know nothing about them. I curse and fume. Somewhere in the house, the ghosts must be laughing their sheets off.

Recently, I was writing at my computer ("Fresh To You From Sunny Mexico"). The kids were at school. My wife was at work. The dog was asleep. The house was blissfully silent. Without warning, a loud whirring commenced behind me. I surveyed the room's electrical appliances, puzzled that one might've suddenly come to life on its own. Just as I ascertained that the videocassette recorder was rewinding a tape all by itself, the whirring stopped and the machine spit out the tape. Then, the VCR just sat there, its red eyes glowing, the tape protruding like a mocking tongue.

It gave me the creeps. I kept my distance, but the VCR didn't seem to have anything more diabolical on its agenda. After a while, I returned to my work, trying to stifle the notion that the house was possessed. Naturally, I'd lost the thread of whatever I was writing.

After much thought, I concluded the boys must've left the VCR running. It reached the end of the tape, automatically rewound, and upchucked the tape. No mystery after all. But the kids denied ever using the VCR. And, if they didn't do it, then we're once again faced with the specter of paranormal activity.

I need help from professional ghostbusters. I'm thinking of calling Mulder and Scully. The truth is out there.

DINNER TIME
IS QUALITY TIME

Child-rearing experts tell us it's important that families share meals. Dinner time should be a ritual, they say, a time for gathering together, sharing school news, and discussing current events. A time of glowing cheeks, hot food, and table settings worthy of a Norman Rockwell painting.

In households where both parents work outside the home, such dinners are difficult to schedule. But because I work at home, we usually manage to get the entire family around the table at the same time. Here's what the rest of you are missing.

DAD:	"Damn, I got all sweaty cooking this. What's the temperature in this kitchen? Eighty? Ninety?"
MOM:	"Put your napkins in your laps."
NO. 1 SON:	"Broccoli? I hate broccoli."
NO. 2 SON:	"I'm going to miss my favorite TV show."
MOM:	"Eat it. It's good for you."
NO. 2 SON:	"If I eat real fast, can I go watch my show?"

DAD:	"Eat the broccoli. You want to get colon cancer?"
MOM:	"Let's not discuss colons at the table. Put your napkins in your laps."
DAD:	"I'm sweating onto my plate."
NO. 1 SON:	"If he eats my broccoli for me, can we both go watch TV?"
DAD AND MOM:	"*No!*"
NO. 2 SON:	Whimpering noises.
DAD:	"Enough. How was everyone's day?"
MOM:	"Is that your napkin? Why is it on the floor?"
NO. 1 SON:	"The dog *likes* broccoli."
DAD:	"I had a good day. How about the rest of you?"
NO. 2 SON:	Gargling noises.
MOM:	"Don't gargle your juice."
NO. 1 SON:	"My day sucked."
DAD:	"Don't say 'sucked.' It's rude."
NO. 2 SON:	Choking noises.
NO. 1 SON (UNDER HIS BREATH):	"Sucked, sucked, sucked."
NO. 2 SON:	"Does anybody care that I'm choking to death?"
MOM AND DAD:	"*No!*"
MOM:	"Mine went okay. But I was in meetings all day. I'm exhausted."
DAD:	"You look tired."
NO. 2 SON:	"*Pikachu! Pikachu!*"
MOM:	"What do you mean, I look tired?"
NO. 1 SON:	"A girl tried to kiss me today."
DAD:	"Nothing. I mean, you said you're exhausted. Your eyes are droopy."
MOM:	"Don't put your face down to the plate. Lift the food on your fork."

DAD:	"Kiss you? What did you do?"
MOM:	"What do you mean, droopy?"
NO. 2 SON:	"Do you like seafood?"
MOM AND DAD:	*"No!"*
	No. 2 Son opens mouth so we can all "see" the "food" inside.
NO. 1 SON:	"Gross! You're disgusting!"
MOM:	"Don't call your brother disgusting."
NO. 2 SON:	"Droopy eyes! Droopy eyes!"
MOM:	"Don't be disgusting."
NO. 1 SON:	"I kicked her."
DAD:	"Who?"
MOM:	"What did you do all day?"
NO. 1 SON:	"The girl. Miss Kissy-face."
MOM:	"Don't kick people. It's not nice."
NO. 1 SON:	"At least it's not disgusting. What is this meat?"
DAD:	"The usual. Wrote a column. Laundry. Vacuumed the floors."
NO. 1 SON:	"I'm not eating this. Here, boy. Here, boy."
DAD:	"Don't drop that on my clean floor."
NO. 2 SON:	"May I be excused?"
MOM:	"Get that dog away from the table."
DAD:	"Here, boy. Here, boy."
DOG (CONFUSED):	"Arf! Arf!"
MOM:	"You don't want seconds?"
NO. 1 SON:	"I didn't want firsts. Did Dad cook this?"
DAD (BRISTLING):	"Yeah, what about it?"
MOM:	"It's very good. Eat it."
NO. 1 SON:	"Sucks."
DAD:	"Where did the other one go?"
MOM:	"He excused himself to go watch TV."

DAD:	"You think he tastes anything when he eats that fast?"
NO. 1 SON:	"I hope not, for his sake."
MOM:	"You're excused, too."
	No. 1 Son departs, grumbling.
MOM:	"Alone at last. That seemed to go well."
DAD:	"Another successful family dinner. Is it hot in here?"

FAMILIAL COMMUNICATIONS, PART I: THE KIDS

My two sons, like most children, have a special sign language they use when they think parents aren't looking.

Talking back gets them in trouble, but they have a better chance of getting away with a nonverbal retort. And if the other brother happens to be watching, all the better. They dissolve into titters, prompting the following transaction.

DAD (WHEELING AROUND):	"What's so funny?"
BOYS (IN CHORUS):	"Nothing!"
DAD (SUSPICIOUS):	"Okay."

They think we never see them, and mostly we let them think that. Part of the parental strategy at our house is letting the boys unite against us. It gives them a common ground. Brothers should be close.

I remember making faces behind my parents' backs when I was a kid. They were mostly the same grimaces and gestures, coming from the Catalog of Universal Kid Misbehaviors. My kids resemble me enough that, when I catch them pulling faces at me, I can see myself there. It's unsettling.

Here, for you inexperienced parents or for those with poor

peripheral vision, is a primer to the gesticulations that are going on when they think you're not watching.

THE EYE ROLL
No, this is not something you get in Asian restaurants. It's that well-practiced optical gesture all children have mastered. It can be used to indicate many emotions, most of which translate to: "My parent is an idiot."

THE SHRUG
Only works if a sibling is watching. Says, "Who knows what parents are thinking?"

THE FROWN
More than the common unhappy expression. This one's exaggerated until the child resembles the sad clown at a circus. Used to express grief over whatever parent has just suggested. Most common reaction to "Go clean your room."

THE GAG REFLEX
When parents say something particularly square or stupid, children clasp their hands to their throats, stick out their tongues, and make gagging noises. Even parents think this is funny—the first time. After a hundred or so times, you want to put your own hands around the child's neck.

FLAPPING LIPS
Children enjoy repeating whatever insipid command a parent has just issued. They do this without making a sound. They twist their lips around, then patter them together to mimic moronic parent. Think of Chevy Chase on the old *Saturday Night Live* news show.

THE TONGUE
Every defiant child has stuck out his tongue at a retreating parent. It's a primitive challenge, a satisfying flaunt to authority. If busted, child faces mandatory solitude.

Many creative children come up with unique ways of expressing frustration. Creativity should be encouraged.

My older son expresses anger this way: his hands curve into claws beside his hips. His face turns red. He starts huffing and puffing. He looks like the big orange monster in Bugs Bunny cartoons. Which, come to think of it, is probably where he got it. Laughing at him only makes it worse.

Son No. 2 can roll his eyes back in his head until only the whites show. Add in sunken cheeks and a protruding tongue and it's a particularly gruesome visage. That one can scare me if I suddenly turn around. Flashback to Linda Blair in *The Exorcist*. Or KISS.

THE PARENTAL RESPONSE

Parents devise many ways to react to these childish displays.

Some parents make faces right back, but this is not recommended. It only encourages bad behavior, and it can frighten smaller children and result in future psychiatrist fees. Others ignore it, figuring it's a normal phase of childhood and will remedy itself before the child reaches college and makes faces at the dean. Some parents clamp down on such misbehavior and remain in constant twitchy vigilance for the next incoming gesture. Some stomp around and yell about "respect," which is what the child was secretly hoping.

Me? I go with the traditional approach. I always say, "Your face is going to freeze like that." And the kids always respond, "Cool!"

FAMILIAL COMMUNICATIONS,
PART II: THE PARENTS

Parents are easy to spot, and not just because they usually look frazzled and sleep-deprived. Their speech patterns give them away.

Even when their children aren't around, parents talk like parents. They say things childless adults never utter.

Parentspeak is largely a product of fatigue and distraction. For parents, life is one big conversation, a constant barrage of prodding, permission-seeking, and Pokémon. It wears us down. We resort to spouting parental clichés because it's easier than being creative. Pretty soon, we're channeling our own parents, singing old standards like: "Well, it didn't just get up and walk away, now did it?"

Being around children all the time is hazardous in another way, too. Their incessant prattle plants seeds in our minds, which later come blooming from our lips as inappropriate adult conversation.

If, for example, a business contact answers your every "did not" with a "did, too," you can bet she's a parent. If a deskmate asks you to catch his phone while he goes to "poop," there's no question he's got small children at home. If a colleague uses the phrase "I'm rubber and you're glue" . . . well, you get the idea.

I've collected examples of parental clichés for your reading pleasure. Be warned, however. None of these phrases should be used in the company of other adults. Never say any of the following in a business setting.

With that caution in mind, here then, are.

THE TOP 50 THINGS
THAT ONLY PARENTS SAY:

50. Use soap.
49. Don't kiss the dog.
48. Where are your shoes?
47. If I were a shoe, where would I be?
46. Hay is for horses.
45. What part of "no" do you not understand?
44. Tickle, tickle, tickle.
43. Tie your shoes.
42. All right, look sloppy. See if I care.
41. Don't sit so close. You'll ruin your eyes.
40. Your socks don't match.

39. It's on your left. No, your other left.

38. Why is the remote control all sticky?

37. When I was a boy, we didn't even have remote controls . . .

36. Turn that down. You'll wake the dead.

35. Hush (try that one on a coworker sometime).

34. Zip it (ditto).

33. Blow on it (don't go there).

32. Use your napkin.

31. Don't shovel your food.

30. Because it builds strong bones.

29. Three more bites.

28. Clean your room.

27. You call this clean?

26. Why do I have to do everything around here?

25. If I hear "*Pikachu*" one more time . . .

24. Stop talking and go to sleep.

23. If your brother jumped off a cliff . . .

22. Aw, get up. That didn't hurt.

21. I'll kiss it and make it better.

20. When I was your age . . .

19. I don't know. I haven't been wearing your shoes, now have I?

18. Close the door. Were you raised in a barn?

17. In or out, in or out. Make up your mind.

16. When you start paying the utility bills around here . . .

15. Stop slamming that door!

14. Money doesn't grow on trees.

13. By the time I count to three . . .

12. Walk faster.

11. Stop running!

10. Don't you run from me!

9. Don't put that in your mouth. You don't know where it's been.

8. Did you go?

7. Get down from there!

6. Somebody's gonna get hurt!
5. Put that down. You'll put your eye out.
4. This is my final warning . . .
3. What's that smell?
2. We'll see.

And, the Number One Thing That Only Parents Say is: "Because I said so."

FAMILIAL COMMUNICATIONS, PART III: THE TOUGH QUESTIONS

I was driving somewhere with my two sons when the younger one asked, "Dad, how does the blinker know which way you want to go?"

I chuckled. My older son smirked. The little one just stared at us. His question was sincere and he wanted an answer. So I explained how the turn signal lever worked—up for right, down for left—and my questioner went "Ahhh," and everybody went away happy.

That one was easy. A softball question. But parents know that children never stop asking questions, and some are much tougher. We feel we must answer, partly because we want our children to grow into educated adults who can support us in our old age, and partly because we don't want to give them further reason to believe we're stupid. The down side is that we don't always know the answers. We slept through class that day. Or college drinking binges killed the brain cells that stored that data. Or our parents fed us bad information when we were kids.

As a public service to parents, I've compiled the following primer with answers to the questions most commonly asked by children. If you'll take a few minutes to memorize this information, you'll be better prepared when your child unleashes some poser, such as, "Why is the sky blue?"

The sky is blue because there's so much water vapor in the air. This is the same reason that the ocean is blue.

Thunder is the sound of God bowling. Yes, He always makes strikes, He's infallible. And He doesn't have to rent His shoes.

There's no such place as Hell, unless you broke Mom's favorite vase.

Heaven does exist and all your dead pets will be waiting for you there. Somebody else has to feed them, just like Dad does here on Earth.

There are no monsters under the bed. Those are dustbunnies and they're harmless.

Ditto for monsters in the closet. All the monsters came out of the closet years ago and now they have an annual Monster Pride parade.

The answer to all questions involving math is "4."

We have to sleep every night so our bodies will get the rest we need and we will grow tall and strong. Also, it's the only time we get any quiet around here.

Dogs lick themselves there because they can.

Yes, it hurts to get a tattoo, and I'll hurt you worse if I ever catch you near a tattoo parlor. Ditto for piercings.

Solar eclipses occur because we have incurred the wrath of the gods. Lunar eclipses are caused by a giant hairball passing between the Moon and the Earth. If you stare directly at either type of eclipse, you'll go blind. I said the gods are wrathful, didn't I?

We must bathe regularly because our bodies constantly shed skin cells and they must be scrubbed away. Plus, we want to keep our friends.

Computers contain a little man who sorts the various programs, keeps them organized, and hands them over when asked. A computer "crash" occurs when the man is sleeping. His name is Intel, and that's why the machine has a sticker that says "Intel Inside."

No, your favorite cartoon characters do not "live" inside the television. TV shows are images beamed from far away. Cartoon characters all reside in Toonville. They're very happy there, even though many are enslaved by an evil genius named Michael Eisner.

Yes, disco ruined popular music. My generation regrets the error.

Superman's X-ray vision does allow him to see through everybody's clothes. No, you can't master that yourself.

Adults kiss because they like each other. The longer they kiss, the more they like each other. If you see a kiss that lasts longer than ten seconds, you should change channels.

Grass feels no pain when it is mowed. It's just like a haircut.

It's okay to stomp bugs. There are plenty more where those came from.

Swallowing watermelon seeds will indeed make watermelon vines grow out of your ears. That's why you must keep your ears clean.

Children who ask too many questions grow bigger ears. And then everybody will see those watermelons in there.

"EXTRACURRICULAR" TRANSLATES TO "PAIN IN THE NECK"

If you're one of those working parents who thrives on pressure, if you just don't have enough stress in your life, then I'd suggest you run right out and enroll your children in some extracurricular activities.

Scouts and sports, science fairs and spelling bees, music lessons and dance lessons, and children's theater all can broaden your kids' horizons, give them life skills, and refine their special talents. And these events can turn you, the parent, into a gibbering idiot.

Careful analysis finds that the strain of extracurricular activities can be divided into three major categories: transportation, practice, and stage fright.

TRANSPORTATION

Once your children become involved in after-school activities, you'll soon recognize the origins of the phrase "drive me crazy."

The parents' main role in these activities is to chauffeur the little hellions, er, geniuses, from one rehearsal/soccer game/club meeting to another until we see city streets in our sleep.

No matter where you live, these events will take place halfway across town. This is so you can't actually go home and get anything done while the kids are attending their activities. You might have enough time to run a quick errand or grab a cup of coffee nearby, but you'd better be back to retrieve your kids at the precise time the activity ends. Otherwise, you'll never hear the end of it.

If you have more than one child, you can count on their activities starting at the same time, miles away from each other. This is why you see so many hysterical "soccer moms" roaring wild-eyed through traffic in their minivans. The kids are in the back seat, repeating in a singsong manner, "We're gonna be la-a-a-ate."

Most activities require special gear—toe shoes, scripts, sneakers, and Scout uniforms. The Murphy's Law of extracurricular activities is that these items will be "lost" every time your children need them, a condition that won't be discovered until you're halfway there. Your best bet is to keep everything in your vehicle at all times. Sure, your car may look and smell like a gym locker, but at least the search will be localized.

PRACTICE

Everyone knows that old joke: "How do you get to Carnegie Hall? By refusing to practice until your parents go insane."

Yes, practice goes against the grain of most children, who saunter around with the innate assurance that they can ace that spelling bee/recital/playoff game without any preparation.

Trying to get kids to practice regularly is a major source of ulcers and baldness in parents. You can nag. You can stand over them. You can recite their lines along with them until you know their parts better than they do. You can pull out all your hair, scream, double over, and grasp your stomach. None of it will do any good. And if you do succeed in getting them to practice, say, the saxophone, then you'll be trapped in the house with them while they squawk and honk like scalded geese.

The solution? Make them practice in the car. All their stuff's out there, anyway.

STAGE FRIGHT

No matter how well you drill your children, when it comes time to actually perform, expect opening-night jitters. Nervous pacing, rumbling guts, nail-biting, and uncontrollable twitching. All on the part of the parents. The kids will be fine, either too confident or too obtuse to recognize the opportunity for humiliation that lies ahead.

Both of my sons have participated in spelling bees lately. One is active in Cub Scouts. The other was in a play (Shakespeare, no less). At these events, the parents were much more anxious than their children. They mouthed lines along with their kids, muttered curses, and recrossed their legs repeatedly, as if they needed to go to the bathroom.

The kids' main reaction? Yawning. Right up there on stage. My wife says this is a nervous reaction, caused by the child's need for extra oxygen. I think it's because they were up too late the night before, cramming with their parents.

Parents can be forgiven all their symptoms of stress. They want their children to perform well, to not be embarrassed. They want home-video moments of successful recitals and sports championships. But mostly, they want to make all that driving pay off.

COMMUTING:
CHILDREN ARE THEIR OWN LITTLE AIR BAGS

For most people, commuting is a daily pain, a harrowing gauntlet of freeway snarls, orange barrels, and moron motorists. One of the joys of telecommuting, you'd think, would be eliminating the drive from your everyday life. But we who work at home sneer at such assumptions. Not only do we drive as much as ever, but we're *never alone* in the car.

When you commute by yourself, you get to pick the radio

station, you get lost in your thoughts, and you can curse the other drivers with impunity. But us? We've got children in the back seat, making demands, twitching and squirming, shouting and squealing, and, God forbid, touching each other.

As we chauffeur the children around, we're at their mercy. They're free to do whatever they want in the back seat because we have to keep our eyes on the road. I remember when I was growing up, my angry father would warn, "Don't make me pull this car over." And my brother and I would giggle and snort because we knew he'd never stop to discipline us, not unless we started a fire. He was too intent on getting the drive finished. Now, I'm the same way.

I've heard all the advice from parenting experts about keeping kids distracted while they're in the car. We play the Slug Bug game wherever we go. For the uninitiated, the game goes like this: you keep your eyes peeled for a Volkswagen Beetle. When you spot one, you shout out, "Slug Bug!" and whack your seatmate on the shoulder. I quickly banned the punching part of the game, but my two sons adapted their own version that includes shouting out the color of the Bug. We also count Slug Vans and Slug Trucks (which include anything with rounded fenders). Often, when things get too rowdy, I'll just shout out, "Slug Bug" and they'll get so busy trying to outnumber my finds that they'll calm down.

Music also soothes the savage brats, and they're particularly fond of oldies, which includes any song recorded before, oh, yesterday. When they're getting loud, I keep turning up the radio, hoping some tune by James Brown or The Temptations will grab their attention. Unfortunately, they're more likely to seize upon some song I can't stand. I'll punch the radio button with muttered disgust only to hear, "No, Dad! Go back! I *like* that song!" Do I oblige? You betcha. Better to listen to Neil Sedaka than to more bickering.

Their tastes aren't all repellent, though they are diverse. Ask my older son his favorite band and he'll answer the Beatles. The younger one likes the Beach Boys and the Spin Doctors. They both know all the words to "Joy to the World" by Three Dog Night and "Walking on the Sun" by Smashmouth. Go figure.

Having kids in the car restricts more than the driver's musical choices. From the back seat, children can eye the speedometer and compare it to speed limit signs whizzing past. A lecture soon follows.

Worst of all, kids inhibit your freedom of speech. You can't comment out loud upon the obvious mental deficiencies of the other drivers. I've always been the type of driver who keeps up a running commentary on what the other idiots are up to, usually in terms that would make a sailor blush. Parents quickly learn to quell this compulsion. The worst word blurted in the heat of a near-miss moment will be the one surely repeated at the dinner table.

A few years ago, I was at a red light, facing one other car. Both of us had our blinkers going to turn left. The light changed and I started making my turn. The other driver, who apparently had decided to go straight after all, stood on his brakes, honked, and made obscene gestures at me.

Instantly furious, I yelled, "You had your blinker on, you mo—"

And then I caught myself, remembering that I had a five-year-old in the back seat. As I chewed off my tongue, the five-year-old said somberly, "Dad, it's not nice to call someone a moron." I said, "That's right, son. Sorry."

And I longed once again for the solo commute.

10.

MY DOG ATE MY HOMEWORK
AND MY SPRINKLERS

It can be a lonely workday for those of us who labor at home, but here's the answer: get a dog.

As I mentioned earlier, we have a dog named Elvis. (Although, by the way leaves and dead grass adhere to his shaggy fur, we probably should've named him Velcro.)

Elvis is the first dog at our house after a ten-year hiatus. Our last pet before him was a mutant Airedale named Scotch, who still thought he was a fidgety lap dog when he reached eighty pounds. Scotch nearly caused me to swear off pets forever. He ruined the yard. He left tooth marks in the doorknob, trying to get inside. He barked all day while my wife and I were at work, prompting the neighbors to leave anonymous threatening notes. I realize now that he was lonely, neurotic, and way too excitable. We found him a nice home before our first son was born.

While that was a terrible experience in pet-owning, it was, I learned later, pretty good training for parenthood.

I wasn't in any hurry to try another dog, but my wife and kids wore me down. My best ammunition—a dog would be lonely and loud if left alone all day—became a dud once I started working at home. So, we adopted a Humane Society puppy. Actually, at seventy-five bucks, it was more like ransom.

My sons say Elvis "ain't nothin' but a hound dog," but I

believe he is part Clydesdale. He nearly doubled in size the first month we had him. We told the boys we got them a pony.

By the time he was full-grown, he was seventy pounds or so with long, twisted dreadlocks. He's built sort of like his namesake, wide in the shoulders and narrow in the hips. He's supposedly half sheepdog and half Scottish deerhound. I didn't know what a deerhound looked like, either, until I looked it up. Long legs, deep chest, and grizzled fur. Bred to actually chase down deer and tackle them like a linebacker. Since dogs typically don't wear shoulder pads, he comes equipped with a set of choppers like a great white shark.

Elvis is rowdy with the kids, apparently thinking they're puppies, which isn't far from the truth. But he thinks I'm the Alpha Male, in charge of things around here (ha, ha!), and his job is to follow me around the house.

When I go to the kitchen for coffee, he comes along, watching carefully, as if he's trying to learn to brew French Roast. (Which wouldn't be a bad trick to teach him, come to think of it.) When I'm working at my desk, he sleeps. He's delighted to go outside and play by himself.

He is, in fact, the perfect coworker. He doesn't talk back. He doesn't complain. He does exactly what is requested of him (sure, that's essentially nothing, but he's good at it). He never tries to sell me band candy. He doesn't goldbrick and then hog all the credit. Indeed, a dog can even provide a good excuse for your own lolly-gagging. This has been true since the days of "the dog ate my homework," though it pays to be more sophisticated than that now. Your grandmother can pass away only so many times, but your dog can have repeated miraculous recoveries.

A dog makes sure you don't sit too long at your desk. You have to let him outside and later you have to let him back inside. He'll let you know when. One way or the other. Get too wrapped up in your work and the carpet suffers.

There are disadvantages. Elvis sheds hairballs, something you don't see much with human coworkers. And humans don't usually snore and drool while you work. Well, some do. But they don't usually "chase rabbits" while they're sleeping. That can be distracting.

Because Elvis follows me wherever I go, I have a good excuse when walking around the house, talking to myself. I'm not really talking to myself like a lunatic, I'm talking to the *dog*. Maybe he doesn't answer, but it helps to have someone to bounce ideas off. I find myself muttering, "Elvis, where did I leave that invoice?" And then, "Ah, here it is!" He shares my delight, naturally, though he may just be scamming for another Milk-Bone.

But the No. 1 reason a dog is best is this: you can rarely get your human coworkers to lie on your feet and keep them warm.

PUPPY POWER,
OR
OOPS, THERE GOES ANOTHER SPRINKLER HEAD

For the first year or so we had Elvis, we put up with the usual puppy misbehavior—chewing up socks, dragging in unmention-ables from the yard, jumping up on people and shredding their hose. The usual stuff, hardly worth mentioning. Fortunately, he's a gentle soul. Bites and the resulting injuries are believed to have been largely accidental.

But he put his giant teeth to use in other, inexplicable ways, the main one being that he ate PVC sprinkler heads. Well, he did-n't eat them exactly. He chewed on them until they looked like shredded plastic daisies poking up from the back lawn. Or, he managed to snap them off their stems altogether, leaving bare white pipes jutting from the ground like broken bones.

For people who work at home, household projects, such as repairing sprinkler systems, are part of our job description. That's fine for those who are naturally handy, the types who always know the right tool to use, who innately understand the geom-etry of pipefitting. I'm not one of those people. To me, household repairs are as complicated as those logic problems they sprang on us in high school, the ones about the two trains traveling from opposite directions at different speeds. I never could grasp those problems. I just sat and waited for the train wreck.

But I've learned about pipes and sprinkler heads. It's an arcane world of male and female threads, reducers, joints, half-rounds, and pop-ups. One row at my local hardware store is filled with wire bins overflowing with all the various parts. You're supposed to sort through these parts until you get the right combination to attach new sprinklers to existing pipes. It's like a giant Rubik's Cube.

Attaching the parts, I learned, requires a special glue. Given all the warnings on the can, it's a wonder the Environmental Protection Agency will let us use it at all. The instructions order you to encase your entire body in protective gear before you open the can. The manufacturer put the lid on so tight, I had to use a monkey wrench to get it open, which resulted in it suddenly bursting open and sloshing on my hand. I expect that hand to fall off any day now.

I got the sprinkler system fixed after only two hours and a third trip to the hardware store for missing parts. Rarely have I been filled with such a sense of accomplishment. Standing in the sunshine, watching the rainbow arcs of water spritzing onto my parched lawn, I wanted to raise my arms and dance about. I wanted to hear the theme from *Rocky*.

It didn't last, of course. Three days later, I returned from a trip, to be greeted by these words from my wife: "We've got another fountain in the back yard." I went outside to find another shredded daisy. Elvis stood nearby, not looking the least bit sheepish. He seemed proud, in fact, as if he'd accomplished something wonderful against all odds. Maybe we should've named him Rocky.

DOGS, LIKE KIDS, LEARN TO DO BETTER— EVENTUALLY

You always hear people say their pet is "one of the family." At our house, the question is which one?

We have three boys at our house, including Elvis. All three

have more or less human names. How come, when I go to shout for a boy, I call the dog's name? I've even caught myself calling Elvis by the boy's names occasionally. Am I slipping?

I think it's because the three of them act about the same—rambunctious, loud, needy, and prone to spurts of intense energy. And they're all roughly the same size, though Elvis has a lot more hair. When I address them, my tone of voice is often the same—a weary, scolding, I-caught-you-and-I-can't-believe-you-did-that baritone. It's the principal's voice. It works on dogs. Not so well on boys.

Now that he's been around a while, the boys can't remember Life Without Elvis. I remember, and they're fond memories. I remember being able to walk around barefoot. I remember when dustbunnies weren't fed by dog hair until they were the size of tumbleweeds. But I admit Elvis has become part of the family, just as everyone predicted. And I spoil him as bad as the others do. Working at home, I spend more time with him than with anyone else. No wonder his name is the first to come to my lips.

I'm responsible for much of the day-to-day training for him and the boys. Sometimes, it feels as if I'm talking, talking, talking all the time, trying to teach the three of them, trying to make them understand how the world works, trying to get them to stop spilling everywhere. The instruction of Elvis is going well. A lot of the hardships—disappearing sprinkler heads, for instance—was puppy misbehavior. Elvis has outgrown them now, just in time to save himself from finding "a good home." He's gotten smarter as he's aged, too, something you can't always say for humans.

He's learned all the basic tricks (except "roll over," which makes him laugh) and shows an amazing grasp of English. Ask him what he wants, and he'll make you follow him to the back door or to an empty water dish. Give him a complex command— "Go get your bone and bring it in the house"—and he'll figure it out. It's like having Lassie around. I spend a lot of time saying, "What is it? What is it, boy?" I fully expect him to inform me that little Timmy has fallen down the well.

My wife even taught him to do a chore. (It was about time he started pulling his weight around here. He can't spend all his time sleeping, sniffing, and licking, can he?) She taught him to fetch the newspaper from the yard. Now this was a bold concept because it involved the potential freedom of the unfenced front yard. There was a good chance Elvis would zoom out the door and never come back, too busy sniffing other dogs and licking joggers. But within a couple of days, my wife had him fetching like a champ.

My wife usually handles Elvis's wake-up call because she's the first one out of bed. My own experiences in the milky dawn have been mixed. The first time I tried it, the fat Sunday paper was in one of those slippery condoms to keep it dry. Elvis grabbed the plastic bag in his teeth and sprinted back to the front door. Unfortunately, he had the bag by the wrong end. Inserts, travel sections, and Parade magazine were strewn behind him all the way across the yard. The second time I sent him on his mission, the newspaper wasn't immediately visible (a car was in the way), so Elvis dashed across the street and brought me the neighbor's paper. Inventive, but larceny nonetheless. I had to tiptoe across the street in my pajamas and put it back.

Just the kind of thing I'd expect my boys to do, if I'd ever taught them to fetch.

ELVIS HAS LEFT THE GROOMER— DON'T LAUGH

I took a black dog to the groomer and came home with a gray one. No, it wasn't a pet swap (though that might not be such a bad idea). When the groomer cut away my dog's black coat, it turned out he was gray underneath. It was as if he'd changed clothes.

The second winter Elvis lived with us, we ignored the state of his long coat, knowing that we'd get it all whacked away so he'd be cool in the summer. By the time I finally got around to taking him to the groomer, he was covered in nappy dreadlocks. After the requisite lecture on taking better care of our pet's coat, the nice lady at the grooming "salon" told me to come back for

Elvis in nine hours. Removing a winter's worth of dreadlocks, it seems, is an all-day sucker.

"One thing," she said as I was departing. "When you pick him up, you can't laugh."

Huh?

"Promise you won't laugh. It'll embarrass him. He'll think he's beautiful."

I promised, though the mere thought of such a pledge made me giggle. You want someone to laugh, all you have to say is, "Don't laugh." Comedians could use that approach and save the effort of coming up with jokes.

By the time I went to pick him up, I was chortling uncontrollably. The thought of Elvis, so shaggy and huge, suddenly shorn of his Samson-ite locks, was guaranteed to be a laugh riot. And I'd been admonished not to laugh and, well, you get the idea.

I was a few minutes early, so I peeked around the corner into the grooming area and there was Elvis (at least I thought it was Elvis) up on the grooming table, his neck in a noose, scissors snipping away at his legs. The groomer spotted me and—get this—clapped her hand over Elvis's eyes.

"We're not ready!" she shouted. "Don't let him see you. And stop laughing!"

I ducked around a corner and waited, trying to get myself under control. I'd only gotten a glimpse, but one thing was sure: there was a lot less dog now than when I'd brought him in that morning.

Under all that matted hair, it turned out, Elvis is a skinny dog. Built kind of like a greyhound, with long, spindly legs no bigger around than a spool of thread. And he's gray. The groomer left his beard and mustaches long, so his face looks boxy and professorial. He doesn't look like my dog at all. He looks like a Schnauzer on stilts.

I managed to keep a straight face as he was delivered to me. Writing the whopping check to the groomer helped me remain sober.

Then we went home, where my family had been warned not to laugh at the dog. They fell all over themselves, laughing their tails off. Elvis was abashed, sure, but he's a lot cooler now, and he's grown accustomed to drawing chuckles wherever he goes. He carries his head high, still thinking he's beautiful.

INDOOR WILDLIFE
KEEPS YOU HOPPING

A Sunday morning around dawn. I'm the first one awake. I pad into the kitchen to make coffee, my eyes barely open, the light dim. And a huge brown toad hip-hops across the tile floor.

The following thoughts flit through my mind in seconds: Holy Minerva, a *rat!* No, a toad. A fat toad loose in the house. Quick Sunday School flashback to a plague of toads. But there's only one here. And it looks familiar. Oh, yes, it's the toad my sons have been carrying around in a jar. They named him Billy. He's escaped. Somewhere, a jar lies open, its grass and dirt spilled on the carpet. There he goes. I should catch him. Drat, he went behind the washing machine. Quick, put the dog outside before he eats the toad and spends the rest of the day yarking on the carpet. Where's the jar? Where are the boys? Where's the toad now?

I caught him, of course, though it took on the proportions of a safari before he was finally back in his jar, hopping and banging his head on the lid. Guess that's how he escaped, and he was going with what worked for him before. Not a lot of other options if you're a toad and you have a brain the size of a lentil. It's not like he was going to start tying sheets together to shimmy out a window.

Later, I persuaded the boys to free Billy. They found a nice home for him in the side yard, where the local insects congregate. I'm sure Billy is very happy there.

Having two boys at our house means we have a revolving menagerie of animals living in jars, buckets, and boxes. Boys are irresistibly drawn to wildlife. Billy's only the latest victim, er, specimen.

The experiences haven't always been pleasant, even if they are educational. A few years ago, the boys nursed along a whole bucketful of tadpoles, watching them sprout legs and slowly grow into tiny toads. Then a horrific thunderstorm pounded most of the little amphibians into the mud. The funerals lasted all day. Only one toad survived—the boys named him Billy—and he escaped a few days later, causing tears, worry, and grief.

Then my eldest wanted a box turtle. I bought one at a store and built a makeshift pen in a corner of the yard for him. They named him Speedy. Within days, he'd escaped, never to be seen again, though we spent countless hours probing the shrubbery for him. I told the kids they should've named him Houdini. They didn't think that was funny.

A week or so before the new, improved Billy arrived at our house, the boys briefly enjoyed the company of a full-grown horned toad they found near their grandparents' home. They named him Squint. He was a big hit at show-and-tell at school. Then my sons set his bucket outside so Squint could catch some rays. They put a brick in the bucket so he'd have a warm place to recline. Using the brick as a ramp, Squint did an Evel Knievel out of the bucket and was gone. Tears, fears, and worries that the dog would eat Squint. I found Squint two days later, while mowing the lawn. Fortunately, I got him before the mower did. I returned Squint to the boys with the condition that they free him soon so he could live happily ever after. They gladly complied. It's okay, apparently, to free a beast so he can return to the wild. But if he escapes on his own, it's an insult.

I've resigned myself to the idea that there will be animals in the house, thumping, scritching, and begging to be set free. Since I'm the at-home parent, it'll sometimes fall to me to feed them, free them, or find them running loose. I've only insisted on one rule: no snakes. I'm terrified of snakes, a product of growing up in Arkansas, where there's a poisonous viper every six feet or so. The boys bring a snake into the house, and that's the day I head for the hills, hopping and banging my head against the door until I escape.

INSECT LIFE
DRIVES ME BUGGY

My older son came to me one morning and somberly announced, "We've got to move."

This came as a shock, considering that we'd only recently moved into this house.

"We can't move," I sputtered. "We just got here. Why do you want to move?"

"I was brushing my teeth and I looked in the mirror and there was a spider in my hair."

The spider didn't bite him or harm him in any way, but the alarm of finding a spider in such close proximity was enough for him to surrender the house.

We live in the Rio Grande Valley and the lush greenery means we have lots of insect life, including mosquitoes that swarm at dusk, bumblebees in the shrubbery, and fat houseflies that buzz loops around the porch, waiting for someone to open the door so they can come inside. Grasshoppers, praying mantises, and invisible aphids scurry around our flowerbeds, eating our plants and each other. And we must have a lot of cobs, too, because I keep finding cobwebs everywhere.

Then there are the cicadas that leave their empty husks clinging to every surface. Elvis eats the cicada shells. He'll be loping along and he'll spot one on the wall, and come to a screeching halt. He'll snatch it off with his teeth and crunch-crunch-crunch, it's gone. We've theorized that he thinks they're pork rinds.

My wife and sons made an art project out of cicada husks. They collected a dozen of them and spray-painted them bright blue. I wish they'd warned me first. I discovered the blue bugs clumped together in an ornamental tray and nearly had a heart attack.

Most of the time, we try to adopt a live-and-let-live attitude toward the insect world, but occasionally they get to be too much of a nuisance. Spiders in one's hair, for instance. That's just going too far.

I was sitting at my desk recently, talking to my wife on the phone, when a housefly decided the Garden of Eden resided inside my mouth. He flew right at my face, aiming for my flapping lips. I waved him away and kept talking. He dive-bombed me again. By the fifth time he attempted to land in my mouth, I was screaming, cursing, and waving both arms around madly. My wife, on the other end of the phone line, must've thought I was on fire. I tried to explain the seriousness of the situation, but she was laughing too hard to listen. It probably would've been simpler (and more manly) to just eat the fly.

In most households, it's the man's job to kill and dispose of insects and arachnids who've taken up residence. I try to fulfill this duty, but I'm not as quick as I used to be. Houseflies seem to have radar when I approach with a swatter. They take off before I ever get within reach. I've learned you can throw out your shoulder trying to whack them when they're in mid-air. I even have trouble catching up with spiders. When they make their speedy escapes, I remind myself they have four times as many legs as I do, which helps me feel a little better.

Then there was the war I waged on an anthill in the back yard. I don't mind a few ants running busily around, but this anthill was home to those big red suckers, nearly an inch long. They bite, so they had to go. I drowned the anthill in insecticide, getting a secret little thrill at the way the ants go twitchy, curl up, and die. I puffed out my chest like a Great White Hunter, marched back into the house, and washed my hands thoroughly so I wouldn't go twitchy, too.

Two days later, the ants had excavated a new exit six inches away from the old one and they were back in business. I tried the poisons again, with the same result. I'm sure if I'd looked at the ants through a magnifying glass, their little faces would've been smirking at me.

I finally gave up. Live and let live. We can always move.

11.

Home Repairs,
or
Who's Been Monkeying with My Wrench?

When you work at home, your house is your coworker. And, like coworkers everywhere, sometimes it'll turn on you.

You'll be working along, trying to hit some deadline, when the house will offer some minor distraction or major catastrophe. Next thing you know, the workday's shot. You've accomplished nothing. The house wins again.

Houses apparently are capable of gobbling up possessions. No matter how neat and austere your home, it's full of hiding places. And, inevitably, the thing you need the most will be the one that's gone missing.

A silly example: at our house, we have (conservative estimate) seventy-two sets of nail clippers. So how come when I get a hangnail, all of them have disappeared? The house has swallowed them, that's why. I stumble around, the offending fingernail held high, searching for the clippers. The house cackles maniacally while my work hours disappear.

Office supplies should stay put. We keep them in a central location and we use them frequently. But invariably a particular item will disappear the minute we need it. The household has pilfered it, just like those coworkers at regular offices, the ones too lazy to round up their own supplies.

Children are unwitting accomplices to the house's evil ways. They think nothing of walking off with pens, envelopes, and stamps that the at-home worker will need desperately the next day. I don't care how many paper clips you buy, you'll have none when you need them, particularly if your children have discovered magnets.

I spend most of my work day at the computer, the house blissfully silent because my two sons are in school. But occasionally the house will emit a funny noise. Water running somewhere. Creaking floorboards. The sigh of old masonry as it settles. Next thing I know, I'm wandering around, trying to identify the cause of the noise. And God help me if I find the source. Because that usually means I've got a household repair to do, one that will eat up my day while the work piles up.

Here's an example: I'm at my desk, dutifully writing, when I hear water singing in the pipes. Never a good sign. Up I jump to hustle around the house, checking the faucets, the toilets, and the tubs. No water, water anywhere. I shrug, return to my desk, and try to concentrate on my work. But I can still hear water running. Maybe it's coming from outside. I search for my shoes (the house having hidden one of them), get them on and go out in the yard. Check all the sprinkler valves. They're off. Scratching my head, I make a circuit of the house, hunting the outdoor faucets. Sure enough, one has developed a sudden leak. Water is spraying out around the edge of a large nut that holds the faucet together. Okay, this is the source of the noise. But what to do about it? Surely, I just need to tighten that nut. Leak will stop, noise will vanish. Problem solved.

My work completely forgotten now, I go to the garage and rummage through the toolbox until I find my (carefully hidden) crescent wrench. Then it's back outside. I squat in front of the faucet, adjust the wrench to the nut. One quick half-turn and the problem should be fixed. I barely touch the nut with the wrench when (you guessed it) the faucet explodes apart. Water sprays over me with the same force as a firehose.

I scream and dance backward to avoid the icy stream. Then it's out to the street to shut off the water, into the house to change clothes, and off to the hardware store to buy a replacement faucet.

By the time the repair is made, the sun is setting. And my work remains unfinished on my desk.

What's the answer to house-as-distracting-coworker? I don't know. It's not like I can complain to my boss or request a transfer. Maybe I'll buy some earplugs to block out the house's interference. Several sets. Because you know they'll turn up missing.

HOME REPAIRS ARE JOBS FOR REAL MEN—
COULD SOMEBODY CALL ONE?

A recent TV ad shows a woman desperately phoning locksmiths because her husband accidentally locked himself in the bathroom. As with most clever advertising, I have no idea what they were selling. I only remember chuckling the first time I saw it because the guy was killing time by putting some kind of green cosmetic goo on his face.

Advertising and the media in general portray the American male as being inept. We can't fix anything around the house without causing a minor explosion. We're embarrassed to talk to our kids about sex. We wear stupid "Kiss the Cook" aprons while charring burgers on smoky backyard grills. We think Air Guitar is a spectator sport.

Okay, you're saying, so where's the fallacy in all that? Well, I reply huffily, this stereotype omits a huge chunk of the male population, those savvy types who know how to fix things. Handymen, plumbers, locksmiths, carpenters, boxing promoters. Some men are never more comfortable than when presented with a knotty problem to solve.

I'm not one of those men. Faced with an emergency repair around the house, I curse, mutter, and fume. I make feeble attempts that usually result in skinned knuckles and a worse problem, maybe even a minor explosion. I've learned that the best tool to use in times of crisis is a ballpoint pen—for writing the check to the real repairman who rides to our rescue.

A case in point: we recently needed a locksmith because a

bathroom door was locked and we had no key. Unlike the TV commercial, no one was locked in the bathroom. We were all locked out. One of my sons slammed the door behind him as he exited, the latch caught, and we were stuck. Might not seem like much of a crisis, especially since other bathrooms were available for the most urgent reasons people need a bathroom. But this was the master bathroom, which contains all the cosmetics, hair dryers, razors, and magazines. We needed in there.

I write crime novels in which people are always picking locks. They insert a couple of little metal doodads, give them a twist and—voila!—the door opens. The real world doesn't work that way. After twenty minutes of scratching up the doorknob with Allen wrenches and straightened paper clips, I called the locksmith. He arrived at our house, went directly to the door and, using a gizmo that looked like a pistol with a nail jutting from the barrel, had the door open in one minute flat. I wrote him a check for forty-two dollars.

An hour later, our excitable dog mistook a large plate-glass window for an exit. The window shattered, surprising Elvis and everyone else in the house. The dog was unharmed, but jagged shards went everywhere. After the initial shock, I was pretty calm. Here was a repair job I knew I shouldn't even attempt. Phone calls were made. Repairmen arrived. We wrote a check for two-hundred dollars and the window soon was good as new. The dog forgot all about the trauma. We put a potted plant in front of the window as a preventive measure. Next time, when Elvis heads that way, maybe he'll stop to smell the flowers before lunging through the glass.

We were so grateful for the quick repair that the cost didn't even matter (much). That's the way it usually is when repairmen are summoned. We're just happy that someone, somewhere, has the know-how to fix the sudden leaks and the nights without heat.

And we're not alone. The country is full of homeowners tensely awaiting the next major repair, checkbooks in hand, ready to do our part to support the service economy.

Since I'm the one home all day, I deal with all the repairmen, handymen, and delivery people who come to our house. These guys, who get to see me at home in my rumpled element, tend to snort and squint when I tell them what I do for a living. A real man works with tools, their attitude says, not with words. A real man sure as heck doesn't do all the laundry, clean the house, and tend the children.

Some of them just don't get it at all. One guy was a recent immigrant named Carlos, who registered my occupation with a grunt and a nod. But before he left, he said, "If I need something written sometime, I'll call you." Carlos apparently thought I was running some sort of storefront operation. Rent-a-Writer. I smiled and let him think that. And then I wrote another check.

SITTING AROUND IN MY UNDERWEAR WHILE BLACK GUNK EATS OFF MY HANDS

When we moved into the aforementioned larger house, I noted that it had a flat roof. This is not uncommon here in the Great Southwest, but it was new to me. I didn't pay any attention to the roof until several months later, when part of a torrential rainstorm wound up in my son's bedroom. I decided it was time to get more interested in what's happening up there on top of my house.

A friendly roofing contractor agreed to fix the leak, then gave me simple instructions for maintenance I could do myself, saving two-hundred-and-fifty dollars now and untold headaches in the future.

So, with a can of plastic roof cement in hand, I ventured up a borrowed ladder in search of cracks around the seal between roofing material and parapet. These cracks occur naturally, the roofer told me, a result of heat and cold. Occasionally, you need to go up on your roof and patch them, just to make sure water doesn't find its insidious way inside. At first glance, the seal seemed riddled with cracks. But closer inspection found that most of the grooves weren't cracks at all—they were unsightly stretch marks. I decided to cement over all of them. An ounce of prevention and all that.

If we had stronger truth-in-advertising laws, plastic roof cement would be labeled "Sticky Black Gunk." It's the type of product that makes you say "yuck" when you open the can. Like Spam.

I troweled the gunk onto the seal and it went on easily. In fact, it was sort of pleasurable. It was a quiet, cool Saturday morning and I was up among the trees and the chirping birds. I wondered how many other homeowners around the city were up on their roofs, doing the same job. I felt a kinship with them. We should all be up here, I thought, smearing gunk and waving to each other.

The longer I worked, the hotter it got and the less neighborly I felt. After two hours, all the cracks were dutifully smeared over, I was pouring sweat and my hands were covered with black gunk. Which presented a problem: how to get down off the roof without getting gunk on the borrowed ladder and everything else I encountered?

I'd worn ancient jeans with the intention of throwing them out when I was done, so I wiped some of the excess gunk on them and made my way to the ground, trying not to touch anything with my hands. In the garage, I kicked off my shoes, stripped off my filthy jeans, and padded into the house in my sock feet to clean up.

Uh-oh. Turns out you can't wash black gunk off your hands. Even with cleanser, which I promptly ran out of, anyway. I returned to the garage and (finally) read the instructions on the can. "Clean hands with waterless hand cleaner." Huh? "Caution! Combustible!" Yipes! "Do not take internally!" No problem. "Use protective measures to avoid contact with skin." Big problem.

My wife was out, but was expected to return soon. I couldn't go to the store for waterless cleaner with my hands covered with gunk. I couldn't even put on fresh pants. All I could do was sit and wait, holding my sticky hands aloft like a surgeon who's freshly washed.

Twenty minutes later, my wife arrived. She calmly sized up the situation and hurried to the store to get waterless hand cleaner. I sat and waited some more, itching all over and unable to scratch, certain I could feel the black gunk burning my skin. I pictured my hands red and bubbling underneath the evil gunk. As soon as she returned, I scrubbed off the cement—which took half an hour—to find that my hands were unmarred. I hadn't combusted. I hadn't even gotten the gunk on the furniture or in my hair. Overall, the experience was a success, if you discount the part where I looked like an illiterate, pants-less dork in front of my wife.

The upshot? I'd survived another homeowner's ordeal. I saved two-hundred-and-fifty dollars. And I get to do it all again next year.

PLUMBING 101:
DO YOU HEAR A DRIPPING NOISE?

When you work at home, nothing is more terrifying than the tick-tock of a leaky pipe or the squish of wet carpet.

Plumbing problems are every homeowner's nightmare, but they're particularly horrible for work-at-home types because we're expected to fix them. After all, we're here all day. We've got tools. How difficult can a repair be?

A case in point: recently, one of our toilet tanks developed a drip. I figured I'd put in a new flush valve, seal the fittings tight and—voila!—the problem would be solved. Two hitches with this plan. One, the water line on this particular toilet was made of some inflexible substance—I'm guessing stone—so it would-n't go back where it belonged. And, two, the water line was in a corner, leaving me approximately six microns of space between toilet and wall in which to work.

I did my best, suffering barked knuckles, rug-burned knees, and a storm of frustration in the process, but I couldn't make the leak go away. I ended up calling a professional to finish the job.

(An aside: now, when I order my sons out of the room because I'm watching an R-rated video full of bad language, they say, "Aw, Dad. We heard all those words the day you tried to fix the toilet.")

So, as a service to all of you who work at home, we now offer a Moron's Guide to Plumbing. With these basic instructions, you, too, will be able to tackle any plumbing job. And if you fail, you, too, can call in an expert. Just make sure they don't charge extra for laughing at your attempt.

TOILETS

Maybe it's simple wear and tear, but toilets seem to be the leading cause of plumbing headaches. Toilets are simple. Water comes in through a pipe, stores in the tank and, when you push the lever, flows into the bowl to push what's already there into the sewer pipes. The tank refills and you do it all over again. But if any one of those steps develops a leak or ceases to function, you've got big trouble.

Take a moment right now, while the toilet is working fine, to familiarize yourself with how it works. Lift off the top of the toilet tank and look inside. The first thing you'll notice is that it is exceedingly nasty in there. But don't replace the lid yet. Study the various gizmos inside. Flush the toilet so you can see how it operates. The tall device where the water enters is called the flush valve. The rubber doodad at the bottom of the tank is called the flapper, and it is connected to the gatsby. When you push the flush handle, the gatsby lifts the flapper and—faster than you can say F. Scott Fitzgerald—water flows into the bowl. See how simple?

Attached to the flush valve is the float, a large, bladder-like device on a stick. The float keeps the tank from overflowing. You can adjust the water level by bending the stick. When the stick snaps in two, it's time to make your ninth visit to the hardware store.

SINKS

Sinks are even simpler than toilets, until you try to fix one. Inside the faucet handles are tiny parts called seats and springs. These keep the water from spraying out around the handles. If a leak develops, replace them. If the faucet still leaks, replace them again. Once you've said enough bad words, call a plumber.

Many homeowners save on their water bills by replacing their showers heads with more efficient models. Shower heads supposedly screw on and off with ease, but here's a guarantee—they'll leak when you're done. Better to stick with your existing shower head until the flow is reduced to a trickle. It might take hours to get a decent shower, but better that than a nervous breakdown.

SEWERS

Sewer problems are not for amateurs. If you've developed a severe clog in your sewer line or a sudden sinkhole in your yard, the best step would be to sell the house immediately.

Now that you've been fully briefed, you're ready to tackle any emergency. But keep the plumber's phone number handy, just in case. It helps if you can find one who doesn't laugh much.

GIVING BIRTH
TO A NEW COAT OF PAINT

Painting your house is similar to having a new baby. Years pass, and you forget just how tough it was at the time. You forget the mess, the smell, and the discomfort and remember only the happy glow of the new and fresh. This is why couples have more than one child, and it's why I volunteered to paint my old house.

Painting may be the lowest common denominator of home projects. You might not be able to replace a window pane or service your own furnace, but you can slap paint on something, given the opportunity. Of course, such relative simplicity can be deceiving, leading us to tackle much more than we should. Unrealistic goals lead to slip-ups like the dingy window frames in one bedroom at our old house, overlooked when we last painted and left that way for six years.

Most of our interior then was a color I called "What-Were-We-Thinking Pink," though the paint company called it "Windsor

Rose." It went on our walls the color of Pepto-Bismol and dried to a pale pink that looked fine as long as no light shone directly on it. We lived with that paint for six years and two small boys before we decided it was time for a change.

My wife and I visited the home improvement store, leafed through samples, took home paint chips, and finally settled on a light taupe called "Renoir Bisque." Other finalists included "Sandrock," "Foggy Day," and "Gray Moth." For the woodwork and trim, we chose an enamel called "Pure White."

We also bought rollers, brushes, pans, sponges, yardsticks, and masking tape. We considered one of those power rollers, but the house wasn't that big and, heck, we'd only use it every six years. We got everything home, and I began doing a little prep work every day—scraping, spackling, sanding, and scrubbing.

Six years before, my wife and I had painted the house together, but this time, I was doing it mostly alone. As a house-husband, I had vacant days to concentrate on the paint job and really do it right.

It took a month.

Partly, that's because I could only apply paint when the boys were at Grandma's house. Kids and wet paint don't mix. Partly, it's because I spent an enormous amount of time edging everything in miles of masking tape, trying for crisp edges around the ornamental woodwork. I went back to the store three times for more tape. My motto: tape it now or scrape it later.

But the main reason it took so long was that I needed to rest a lot. House-painting is like doing aerobics all day long—up and down and back and forth, now s-t-r-e-t-c-h. You use muscles that normally get to just lie around in your arms and legs and shoulders, filing their nails, smoking cigarettes, and waiting for an alarm call. And, let's face it, I'm not as young as I used to be. It had been six years since I'd last hefted a roller. In paint, I learned, there is pain.

Despite the aching muscles, painting can be a Zen experience once you find your rhythm, graceful in its smoothness and economy of movement. In fact, it might be almost pleasurable if it weren't for the paint itself. Why does paint have to be a liquid, subject to the vagaries of gravity and spill? Most of the time, I was covered in Renoir Bisque.

It didn't help that the latex paint appeared a radioactive lavender when it was wet—and I was blithely coating my house with it. It lightened as it dried, ending up just the right shade of taupey tan. I think paint manufacturers make it happen that way to drive us all crazy. Their little joke.

However, it turned out well, and it only took another month or two for my body to recover.

Now that we're in a larger house, I keep all my painting gear in a box in the garage. When the time comes to paint this big mother, I'm getting out the checkbook again.

CHILDREN LEARN FROM HOME REPAIRS— JUST DON'T LET THEM DRIVE

Whenever I whine about how much I chauffeur my kids from place to place, I always hear from some Older and Wiser Parent, who says sagely, "Wait until *they* learn to drive. Then you'll have a whole new set of worries."

That day is still far off, but already I break out in hives every time I think about my easily distracted boys behind the wheel of a ton of speeding steel.

I was reminded of this recently when I took the boys to Home Depot. Usually, I avoid the huge hardware warehouses on Saturdays, when they're overrun with desperate do-it-yourselfers making their third shopping trip of the day because they still don't have the right part. But I decided to brave it because of a household emergency. A kitchen cabinet door had come off in my hand and we were fresh out of cabinet hinges here at the house. My wife was working overtime, so I had to take the boys with me.

I told myself this would be a nice father-son opportunity, a chance to expose the boys to the wonders of tools and the aroma of plywood, a playful time of dodging those beeping forklifts that zip lethally around the store. The boys saw it differently. To them, shopping was a dread interruption in a day already packed full of cartoons and play.

As we entered the store, the older son announced he would push the shopping cart, using that petulant tone that told me: he'll push the cart or he'll be a surly pain in the posterior the whole time. I let him push the cart, but only after numerous warnings about how the store was crowded and he'd have to be careful not to run down any beefy carpenters.

I'd made a list of items we needed at the store, trying to save myself future trips, and the list included a couple of leaf rakes. Soon, my son was weaving through the throngs of frustrated homeowners with long, wooden rake handles protruding from the cart. I scampered around the cart, apologizing to those who were goosed by the rake handles and urgently cautioning my son against putting somebody's eye out. He doggedly hung on to the shopping cart's controls as it bumped into aisle displays and raked hanging items off onto the floor.

At one point, the future flashed before my eyes and I had a vision of myself sitting in the passenger seat of a car, my fair-haired son behind the wheel, that same look of grim determination on his face as he ran other motorists off the road. It was enough to make my heart seize up.

I had the same sensation when I took my boys to a video arcade. They took turns at an elaborate 3-D machine that let them race speedboats through stone-walled canals and around obstacles of all sorts. Both boys approached the game the same way: set the throttle on "bat-outta-hell" and run over anything that gets in the way. Other racing boats, idle fishermen, and the occasional water carnival were all creamed by my sons' boats. When they were done, they boasted about their scores and said to me, "Didn't we do great?"

I replied somberly, "You're never driving a car of mine."

The older son's confident smile faltered. "What about when I get my driver's license?"

"You can have a license when you're thirty," I said. "And you can buy your own car for crashing around in."

He seemed daunted for a second, then the light came back into his eyes. "I want one of those speedboats."

I started to ask him if he planned to live in Venice, but I bit my tongue. Let the youngster dream of driving. Someday he'll be out there on the open road (or canal), whether I like it or not. Let's just hope he doesn't have rake handles sticking out his windows.

For the record, when I went back to the hardware store later that same day, I left the boys at home with Mom. And I didn't even use a shopping cart. I only had to buy one small item—the correct hinge for that cabinet door.

12.

THE GREAT OUTDOORS:
YOU MEAN THERE'S LIFE OUTSIDE THE HOUSE?

When you work at home, it's just a short jaunt to agoraphobia.

Agoraphobia—from the Greek for "there are teenagers wearing baseball caps backward in my neighborhood"—is the fear of open spaces. It is a serious psychological condition and not something to be taken lightly. Typically, people with agoraphobia tend to stay indoors rather than risk the panic attacks brought on by exposure to crowds.

People who work in home offices are prime candidates for agoraphobia. We're spoiled by our solitude. We've built cozy nests for ourselves, and we manage to do our work via the comfortable distance of telephone and e-mail. We often go days without face-to-face contact with anyone other than immediate family.

But sometimes we must leave the house and go outside. Then we are reminded that the world is populated by vast numbers of other humans, most of whom seem intent on getting in our way.

I sometimes find myself sounding like a Jerry Seinfeld routine, "Who *are* these people? Don't they have *homes*? Why are they all bent on sharing the same street/store/school/parking space that I want to use? And why are they so rude?"

As I write this, I'm still stewing about a traffic incident. A man pulled out in front of me in a car the approximate size of an Amana refrigerator. Apparently, the vehicle was foot-powered, like on *The Flintstones*, because it took him several blocks to reach a cruising speed of fifteen miles per hour. Then, when we reached a green light, he stopped for no apparent reason. After carefully checking both ways, he proceeded on the yellow light, leaving me sitting at the red, sputtering curses.

Minutes later, I entered a supermarket, only to find the same man wandering the aisles. I wanted to tell him off, but he had twitchy eyes and was dressed like a terrorist. I bit my tongue, collected my groceries, and moved to the slow-moving checkout line. A woman behind me with wild, bottle-blond hair kept screeching about how the store should have more checkers. She was late, she protested. It was the store's fault. And there was the implication that I should just move my overflowing cart and let her get on with her busy, busy life. I paid my tab, avoiding all eye contact, and hurried away.

Then it was on to the bank, where I stood in the velvet-rope maze with a man who had some skin condition that made him scratch himself repeatedly. I got itchy just looking at him. The guy in front of me apparently had never been to a bank before because he questioned every aspect of the transaction. The teller was very patient. I wasn't.

By the time it was all over, I just wanted to go home, unplug the phone, and curl up under a blanket for, say, three days. Agoraphobia, here I come.

I wasn't always such a hermit. When I had a 9-to-5 job, I was downright gregarious. I talked to strangers every day. But working alone ruins you on other people. Now, if someone I don't know speaks to me, my first reaction is: "What's wrong with *that* guy? What does he *want*?" I duck my head and mumble and scurry home.

It's no surprise I turned out this way, I suppose. When I was in junior high school, the counselors gave all the students a personality test as part of a careers class. The test was supposed to find our aptitudes and help us determine what sort of field we should enter as adults. When the counselor scored my test, the results showed that I was best-suited for a job as a forest ranger or as a lookout in a fire tower. In other words, I should be out in the wilds somewhere, far from human contact, working all by myself.

Other folks who work at home may get lonely. They may miss the camaraderie of the watercooler. But plenty of us are happy where we are, away from the open spaces, avoiding the unwashed masses.

Maybe it's not too late to take up fire-spotting.

HELLO, MY NAME IS—
I FORGET

Sometimes, when we work-at-home hermits go out into the wider world, we run into old friends, strike up conversations, and generally act like we haven't become total social misfits. And we're reminded that other people have lives, too, even if we're too caught up in our own domestic melodramas to keep in touch. Not only that, but they have names, and they expect us to remember them.

Seems like everywhere I go lately, I run into familiar faces. The swimming pool, the supermarket, the bank. All my old acquaintances are out and about, ready with a handshake and a smile. And I have no idea who these people are. I know I should know them. I recognize their faces. Sometimes, I can even put them into context—I know this person from my kid's school, from some party, or from a story I covered back when I had a regular newspaper job. But their names? Gone. Forgotten. Erased from the memory banks.

If people were computers, I could just display an "Insufficient memory at this time" message and go on my merry way. People understand that when it comes from machines. But they expect me—a fellow human—to remember their names, which leads to some awkward conversations, such as the following.

"Hi there. You look so familiar. I know that face, but your name escapes me. Yes, yes, of course. I remember you. You just were out of context. I'm not used to seeing you all dressed up like that. Heh,

heh. That's right, we went to school together. And then there was college. Right. Roomed together, you say? Uh-huh. Then there were those ten years we worked together at the newspaper. Sure. Oh, yeah, I *did* see you last weekend at that cookout. Of course. Sorry. I'm terrible with names."

How did this happen? I'd hate to blame creeping middle age. I prefer not to think about that, though the mirror tells the cruel truth. And I don't want to blame the excesses of my youth, when millions of brain cells gave up their lives to the cause of tequila.

Instead, I'll blame my children.

I trace my memory loss to the moment I chose to become a stay-at-home dad. I isolated myself from the world, working at home and spending most of my time with two young boys. And without regular contact with other adults, I began to forget about them. In particular, their names.

My social circle shrank to the number of guys who can fit around a poker table once a week. One close friend I see regularly, perhaps the occasional lunch out with others, but that's it. The rest of the time, I'm home with the boys, forgetting everyone else. Meanwhile, my sons' social circle keeps growing. As they get older, they make more friends and I'm expected to remember the friends' names. And those friends have parents. And they all have names, too. Most of the parents I know have just given up. Now we greet each other with, "Hi, you're So-and-so's Dad." And we nod, knowing that's enough.

(That brings me to Today's Parenting Theory: the section of the human brain that holds other people's names is erased by high-pitched squeals, such as those frequently emitted by children. Enough yowling around the house, and our brains are washed clean.)

There's one more factor here: I write fiction, so I spend a lot of time with my imaginary friends. More time, actually, than I spend with real, breathing adults. All day long I'm in the company of characters like Bubba Mabry, Felicia Quattlebaum, Otis Edgewater, and Benjamin Dover. (Get it? Ben Dover? Har.) Those names are easy to remember because I made them up.

Maybe that's the answer in the real world, too. I'll invent new names for the people I meet. Give them some moniker I'll be more likely to remember.

So, if you run into me somewhere and I call you "Gertrude Beeblefitz," I'm sure you'll understand. You can call me "So-and-so's Dad."

BIRDS OF A FEATHER
CONGA TOGETHER

Lonely workers need the occasional people bath. We need to renew acquaintance with the human race. We need interaction with strangers, the ritual exchange of business cards, and the subtle rush of quick flirtation. We need an excuse to gab, drink, smoke, repeat bad jokes, and make exotic wagers.

To meet these needs, the American business community has invented the convention.

Traditional weekend conventions give people an opportunity to get away from their humdrum jobs for a while. Out of the cubicle and into the larger world, where friends are made, new careers are found, and hearts are broken. Occasionally, some work even gets done. And it's all tax-deductible.

Now, with more than 20 million people working at home, trade conventions have become even more essential to the health of your career. Everyone has to get out there, shake hands, make eye contact, and hope for the best. If you work at home, you need to network so you're not forgotten in your field. If you compete with we who work at home, you'd better attend your industry's conventions because you can bet we homebodies will be there in force. Conventions let us get away from our kids for a couple of days.

A strange transformation occurs when people who work solo attend conventions. Normally, we spend whole days alone, speaking to no one but the dog. We sip coffee and tap away at keyboards, comfortable in our cottage industry. But throw us into a crowd of colleagues and we become back-slapping degenerates—

pouring down liquor, staying up way too late, laughing too loud and talking, always talking. We sit in monkish silence for months, storing up words, so we can spill them in the hotel bar.

During the convention day, we doze through lectures and panel discussions, making the occasional note, which we'll later use as a coaster. We trudge past exhibits and booths. We conduct stilted conversations in hallways with people who'd probably like to have our jobs. All in all, it's like a day at the office.

Everyone becomes more animated as happy hour approaches. Cash bars and evening clothes add an aura of glamour. Hospitality suites beckon. By midnight, we're wearing party hats and leading conga lines around the parking lot.

I recently attended a meeting of mystery writers and fans in sunny Tucson, Arizona. It had been six months since my last convention, and I was pumped up, ready to chatter through a weekend of fun and commerce. I'd even bought new clothes, so I'd look more like a Professional Writer and less like Grizzly Adams.

My hotel room wasn't ready when I arrived because, under federal law, hotels must keep a maid in every vacant room until 5 P.M. With no place to unpack, I had no choice really but to adjourn to the hotel bar. The next nine hours or so were a whirlwind of hand-shaking, book-signing, conversation, and alcohol consumption. That regimen was followed by two more days of the same, interrupted only by fitful sleep, doses of aspirin, and trying to take my pants off over my head. Before I knew it, I was back on a plane, nursing an H-bomb of a hangover.

When I got home, I found my pockets were full of business cards from people I barely remembered and rumpled notes on things I'd drunkenly promised to do—phone calls, interviews, more conventions, whole books—that will take months to deliver, at considerable expense and exertion. And I had a bag full of convention freebies that I woozily gave to my family in lieu of real gifts.

The older I get, the harder it is to bounce back from these weekends of debauchery. I needed extra sleep for three days. My jaws ached from so much unaccustomed yakking.

Then it was back to my desk, back into the hair shirt of

silence, until the next convention draws me out of the house. I hope to be fully recovered by then.

POULTRY IN MOTION

I was nearly killed by a rubber chicken.

My son needed a rubber chicken for a skit he was performing with his classmates. The novelty shop was fresh out, so my wife special-ordered it from wherever they make rubber chickens (rubber plantations?). It was my job to fetch the chicken from the store.

We had a full day's notice that the chicken had arrived, but I put off picking it up. The store was near my sons' school, so I figured we could get it on the way home. But just as I was leaving the house, I realized that my plan involved turning two boys loose in a novelty shop. I decided to swing by the store—alone—*before* I picked up the boys.

I drove quickly, one eye on the dashboard clock, measuring whether I could round up the chicken and still make it to school on time. I hurried into the store, plunked down ten dollars (ten bucks for a chicken you can't even *eat*?), and raced back to the car, bird in hand.

I was cutting it close, and hurriedly weaved through traffic. I was so intent on watching the clock, I didn't see a truck barreling toward me until it was almost too late. Screeching brakes. A quick twist of the steering wheel. Shouted prayers and curses. A near-miss. All because of a rubber chicken.

But wait, you say, it's not the chicken's fault. I was nearly run down by a truck because of my own procrastination. If I hadn't waited until the last minute, I wouldn't have been speeding through traffic. You're right, of course. But the point is that I and, no doubt, millions of other American adults who work at home are constantly rushing from place to place. We have dozens of errands to do and we're always running late.

How does this happen? One reason we choose to work at home is that it allows us to make our own schedules. The day is flexible. We should be able to plan ahead so that our trips out-of-doors are leisurely cruises along our appointed rounds. But we wait until the last possible second, too busy with e-mail, phone calls, and other chores to pull ourselves away. Then we race through traffic, risking our own lives and those of untold numbers of rubber chickens.

Our days are spent rocketing through time and space, trying to get from the dry cleaners to the office supply store to the supermarket and back home again. At every turn, it seems, are slow-moving tourists, road construction, and other obstacles, all conspiring to make us late. If we survive the traffic, we arrive at our destinations harried and breathless, our mouths gaping, our eyes wide. We look, in fact, like rubber chickens.

Repeatedly, I resolve to get an earlier start. Every time, I'm distracted by the clothes dryer buzzing, the phone ringing, or a near-victory at "Free Cell." And then I look at the clock and realize that I have five minutes to make a ten-minute trip. Late again.

I know other work-at-home parents face the same problem. I see them in traffic, teeth clenched, both hands clutching the steering wheel, committing one moving violation after another in an attempt to make up lost time.

The rest of you can help us poor harried parents. Watch for us in traffic. Get out of our way. You don't want to be a victim of our procrastination. And if you see a rubber chicken on the seat next to a stressed-out driver, you might want to drive up onto the sidewalk and wait for the car to pass.

It'll be safer for us all that way.

IT'S NOT SAFE OUT THERE
FOR A LAWN JOCKEY

So I was raking leaves in my front yard on a sunny autumn weekday, careful to always face the street when I bent over so the neighbors wouldn't be exposed to plumber's cleavage, when an older gentleman stopped his sports car at the curb and rolled down his window.

He gave me the hard squint, clearly trying to think of a way to say it, and I figured he was just having a man's instinctual difficulty in asking for directions. But what he said was, "Um, you live around here?" My first thought: no, buddy, I'm raking somebody else's leaves, just for the fun of it.

Then I realized what he was getting at. Here I am in my swank neighborhood, where most people have retirement income and/or real jobs, raking leaves in the middle of a workday. I'm wearing an old flannel shirt, drug-dealer sunglasses, and tattered jeans that I keep hitching up. I don't particularly look like I belong here. This guy thinks I'm the lawn boy.

Now I've got nothing against lawn guys. Most of them probably make more money than I do. It was the gent's assumption that got to me.

I sputtered something like, yeah, this is my house right here. He gave me a dubious smile, then asked his question, and I told him the street he wanted was two blocks over. He waved his thanks and zoomed away, leaving me standing in the yard, frozen in place, pointing like a plaster jockey.

Folks expect a strapping man like myself to be at a job during the week. When they see me doing household business at the bank or the supermarket on a workday, wearing sandals, and with my shirttails hanging out, they assume the worst. They think I'm unemployed. Or that I'm a member of the untaxed shadow economy where the main sources of income are petty theft and crack cocaine. Or that there's something *wrong* with me and any second I might start ranting about government conspiracies and little green men. Or, apparently, that I'm the hired help.

Do other housespouses get this reaction as they go about their daily lives? Do people stare and stammer and avoid the subject of what do you do for a living? Is it just me? Is it my clothes? If I went to the supermarket dressed like Donna Reed, would everyone accept that I worked at home? Okay, bad example. A tall, bearded man wearing an apron and heels to the supermarket probably would get a whole different sort of reaction. But you see my point, right? People are conditioned to expect men (and women, for that matter) to work at a regular job on weekdays. They expect suits and ties. They expect to see us in traffic during rush hour, cellular phones pasted to our heads, stress eating us up from the inside.

Of course, one of the main attractions of working at home is not having to wear the suit and tie. But just because I'm in a bathrobe and sweatpants in the middle of the day, does that make me a crazy person? Okay, don't answer that. Let me put it another way. Does being a slob automatically equate to lower-class citizenship? Is there no room in people's assumptions for househusbandry?

People see a big guy, dressed like Paul Bunyan, walking around in a daze, mumbling to himself about some plot point in a future novel, and they don't think, ah, a literary type, a dreamer. They think: look, it's the wacko who rakes other people's lawns.

Maybe I'm just sending the wrong signals. I guess I could go bohemian, dress in black head-to-toe and sport a beret. But I'm too old and fat to play the starving artist and I have a low tolerance for pretense. I'm planning to make an exception, though. Next time I'm out in the yard, raking leaves, I'm wearing a tuxedo.

LAWN MAINTENANCE MADE SIMPLE— TRY TEQUILA

Lawn care is an important component of home ownership. If you want your property to maintain its value, it's imperative that you keep the grounds in pristine condition. This explains the origin of the term "sweat equity."

Yes, friends, if you've got a yard, then it's time to sweat. It's time to mow, edge, fertilize, and prune. It's time to spend every waking weekend hour with sweat stinging your eyes, exhaust fumes going up your nose, and grass clippings stuck to your socks.

Maintaining a lawn is a form of insanity, particularly here in the Southwest. We pour precious, expensive water on our grass so it will grow. Then we kill ourselves cutting it every week. Then more water. More mowing. More water. More sweat. You get the picture.

The alternative is xeriscaping, which means using less water and keeping your yard in a natural state. Presuming that anywhere in nature exists a landscape of uniform gravel dotted with spiny plants, all underlaid with black plastic.

Some of us prefer the illusion of Eden. We want to walk around barefoot. So we opt for the lunacy of grass.

Lawn work can be maddening. A recent example: I set out to attack weeds in my yard. So vigorous was my attack that the head came off the old hoe I was using. I repaired the hoe and got after the weeds again. Then I went to rake up the victims. The head came off the rake. I fixed the rake, cleaned up the weeds. Then I employed the weed-whacker, which promptly ran out of trimmer line. I took this as a sign that it was time to surrender for the day and go indoors for something cool to drink: a margarita or four.

I once had a neighbor who spent all day, every day, working on his lawn, which was as smooth as a putting green. I couldn't understand why anyone would devote his entire life to maintaining grass. Then I met his wife, and it all became clear. As long as she was indoors, he'd stay outdoors. It was a form of détente.

Most of us, though, don't have the time or the desire to create a perfect lawn. We settle for a yard.

The terms "lawn" and "yard" often are used interchangeably, but they're two very different things. "Lawn" comes from the Latin word for "sweat." On the other hand, "yard" derives from the Anglo-Saxon term for dog poop.

Unclear on which you have? Let's look at the differences.

Lawns tend to be smooth and untouched. Yards have that lived-in look and often feature a car up on blocks.

Lawns have clean edges. Yards have frontiers.

Lawns have ornaments. Yards have stuff.

Lawns tend to be weed-free and to consist of a single species of grass. Yards are inclusive—social mixers where all plants are welcome.

Lawns are a consistent shade of green. Yards feature a broader palette, heavy on browns and tans.

Lawns feel good on your bare feet, but you don't walk on them for fear of bending the grass. In yards, shoes are required, and steel-toed boots are recommended.

If you pay someone to tend your grounds, you probably have a lawn (or, you're getting ripped off).

If you have children and/or a dog, you've probably got a yard. Go out and look at your property. If you find any of the following—dog bones, soccer balls, old socks, used furniture or appliances, mysterious holes in the ground, marbles, frisbees, cigar butts, soda bottles, beer bottles, last week's newspapers, last autumn's leaves, dirty dishes, anthills, termite mounds, fallen tree limbs, dandelions, spurge, cactus, sun-bleached toys, or dead birds—then, my friend, you have a yard.

If you'd like to turn your yard into a lawn, then you must work at it. You must attend to details such as dead birds. You must make sure your lawn-care tools are in good working order. Preparation is the key, and hard, sweaty labor the answer.

A beautiful lawn awaits, Nature's own reward for all your work. But I'd keep a pitcher of margaritas handy, too.

13.

TAKING CARE OF BODY AND MIND,
OR
BETTER LIVING THROUGH NAPPING

One of the drawbacks of working at home is that you can't call in sick.

First of all, there's no one to call. You're it. Unless you want to inform your family and, believe me, they already know. Second, there's no such thing as a day off to be sick when you're the parent-housekeeper-chauffeur-cook-gardener-and-chief-bottle-washer.

Sick days are a luxury reserved for you folks who have regular jobs. Come down with a cold or worse and it means you can stay home and rest. Climb in bed with a fat novel, the TV remote, lots of fluids and snacks, and your favorite over-the-counter medications. Pull the covers up to your chin and sleep all day if you want. No one will expect anything of you. You'll have the sympathy of everyone who hears you're ill. Your family will believe you really are sick because staying home from work is such a rare occurrence. And, most likely, you'll still get paid.

You might worry about the work that's piling up in your absence, but there's nothing you can do about it. The work is at the office. You're at home. Case closed.

We who work at home can pursue days of rest and recuperation (though, most likely, nobody will pay us), but our work remains all around us. The kids still have to be commanded to get ready for school. Meals still must be prepared. Laundry grows into dirty dunes. We lie in bed and watch the work pile up. Every stack of paperwork, every unwashed dish, every dustbunny mocks us, reminding us they'll still be there when we feel like moving around again. In fact, the workload will be worse— paperwork, like dustbunnies, tends to multiply when left unguarded. Somehow, this takes all the fun out of slumping off to bed to tend a fever.

I was reminded of all this recently when I had one of those miserable, nagging colds, the persistent kind that hangs around the respiratory system like juvenile delinquents around a pool hall.

Now I'm no stranger to these colds. Parents can count on our children to bring home all the latest viruses. The colds soon follow. I get two or three a year, and I try to work through them, doping myself with cold medicines and aspirin, waiting them out.

But this particular strain was accompanied by some sort of tropical sleeping sickness. I'd work at my desk for an hour, hacking and spewing, and then I'd have to nap for three hours. Anything physical, such as sweeping, required a full day of bed rest.

Meanwhile, the work mounted up. Deadlines loomed. Dust, dead grass, and dog hair swirled around my feet when I padded into the kitchen for more fluids. Dishes overflowed the sink and began staking claim to the countertops. Toys, comic books, and stray schoolwork buried all horizontal surfaces. I was helpless in the face of this onslaught, too busy sleeping. Between naps, I'd putter around a bit, picking things up, hiding the worst of it, but soon I'd be exhausted and forced to lie very still until I recovered.

The kids were no help. They barely noticed that I was going through a box of tissues a day. They were too busy galloping around the house, strewing toys and filth. My wife made sympathetic noises, but by the fifth or sixth day, I could see it in her eyes when she got home from work: "You're *still* sick?"

So I had no choice but to get well. I arose from my sickbed, took a hot shower, and breathed the steam. I choked down food I couldn't taste so I'd have some energy. I poured down coffee with my Dayquil so I could stay awake long enough to load the dishwasher and round up the dustbunnies.

And you know what? It worked. Soon, I was sleeping only slightly more than a normal person. Order was restored to the house. Deadlines were met. Super Dad was back on track. All was well—until the next virus comes home from school.

TO SLEEP,
PERCHANCE TO DREAM

Sleep deprivation is a serious societal ill, and I'd like to write an informed, persuasive study of it, but frankly I'm too tired to do the research.

I know I've read articles about sleep deprivation, how it causes traffic accidents and irritability and low productivity. The articles are here somewhere, in this landfill I call my office, but I'm too drowsy to hunt for them. Let's just say it's a given: most of us get too little sleep.

We work long hours. We have many worries. Our kids get sick (always, always in the middle of the night). We cut back on sleep to squeeze in leisure activities, visit the gym, or start a second career. And we shuffle around all day like zombies, our eyelids heavy, our bodies weary, our skulls filled with pudding.

It's become a point of pride in our culture to keep going on little sleep. People brag about giving up sleep so they can be more successful. They're getting ahead because they're busily toiling while their competitors snooze. Profiles of business and political leaders always mention how the dynamos work eighteen hours a day and sleep only three hours a night. (Which explains a lot about the bad decisions those business and political leaders make.) The message is: they're too busy pursuing their dreams to waste time on actual dreaming.

For those of us with home offices, the temptation to work instead of sleep is particularly keen. The work's right there, handy, calling to us. We lie in bed, our thoughts unreeling toward sleep, and we get an idea. Or, at least, an inkling that might be a good idea in the light of day. We drag ourselves out of bed and tiptoe to the computer, just to write it down, so we'll remember to pursue it later. Next thing you know, it's sunrise.

I've been a lousy sleeper my whole life. I was one of those kids who read with the flashlight under the covers. For years, through my teens and twenties, I had trouble nodding off at night, so I filled those sleepless hours with more productive activities, such as partying.

Now that I'm middle-aged, I don't have any trouble falling asleep. In fact, I often have trouble staying awake. Most nights, the 10 P.M. newscasters are wasting their breaths. By then, I'm slumped on the sofa with my mouth hanging open.

My problem is that I can't *stay* asleep. I'll saw those logs for a few hours, but then something—the dog, a dreaming child, a distant siren, my own insanity—will awaken me. It'll be, say, 3 A.M., the most absolutely wrong time a person can be wide awake, coming at it from either direction. And I'm lying there, feeling like the only guy in America who's not asleep. I burrow back into the covers, desperate to squeeze in a few more hours. I toss, I turn. I'm too hot, but my feet are cold. I can't stop thinking about that stupid thing I said the other day. Toss, turn. I've got to get busy tomorrow and make that deadline. And the kids are going to the dentist. Can't forget that. Toss, turn. Is the furnace making a funny noise? My brain has started its day, whether my body likes it or not. And there's always work I could be doing. I might as well get up.

So I arise and get busy. And I go around sleepy, grumpy, and dopey all day, making mistakes, bumping into furniture, and saying something stupid that can become my new obsession the next time I'm lying awake. So far, this pattern hasn't made me a dynamo. If anything, I'm so sleepy all the time that my waking and dreaming worlds collide. I dream about work. I fall asleep at my desk. I get mixed up about whether somebody actually told me something or I just dreamed it. Whole days seem like nightmares. I fully expect to wake up someday and find myself faced with the final exam in a college course I've never attended. Naked.

Then, all my dreams will have come true. And maybe I can get some sleep.

THE FIDGETER'S GUIDE
TO EXERCISE

Scientists recently reported that people who fidget gain weight at a slower pace than those who know how to sit still. Apparently, repeated small movements, like toe-tapping and knee-bouncing, burn calories faster than accepted forms of exercise, like running or cycling.

These scientists deserve a big sloppy kiss from those of us who spend long hours sitting at desks. We now have scientific proof that swivel chairs are just as good for working out as expensive exercise equipment. It also gives us a handy excuse when our spouses wonder why we're so tired in the evening: "Not tonight, hon, I've spent a long day fidgeting!"

Many of you may not understand the complexities of fidgeting as exercise, so I'll prescribe a series of exercises aimed at toning and fat-burning. If you follow this regimen faithfully, and eat a balanced diet, you are guaranteed to feel better, look better, and smell better. You'll soon be the envy of those misguided souls who believe sweating is a good thing.

THE BASIC FIDGET

This exercise, while seemingly simple, can be difficult to master. But it's important that you learn it well so it comes naturally. You don't want to strain something. You'll find, once you master the basic fidget, that you'll be able to do it without even thinking about it.

The secret to the fidget is to keep at least one part of your body in motion at all times. This can be as simple as tapping the floor lightly with your foot, or as complex as typing, chewing gum, and jiggling your knees all at the same time. Again, remember to start slowly. You don't want to injure yourself. It's easy to become discouraged when your exercise program is interrupted by a painful tendon or spleen.

Once you've mastered the Basic Fidget, it's time to move on to more strenuous exercises.

THE COFFEE MUG LIFT

This exercise will build your arm muscles, but it does include an element of danger. How many of us have had our workouts (not to mention our workdays) ruined by hot coffee spilled in the lap? Unless the coffee is from a fast-food joint and you stand to make millions off a lawsuit, it's better to keep the coffee in the cup.

Lift the coffee mug slowly to your lips and sip from it. Then set it down on a nearby horizontal surface, preferably one at some distance from expensive computer equipment. Once you have the basic coffee-drinking movement down pat, you can increase the resistance by using bigger mugs. Some of us more experienced desk jockeys have worked up to mugs that hold ten or twelve ounces. But be warned, this is not for the novice.

Important: remember to switch hands occasionally. You don't want one arm to become more developed than the other. This looks odd and can prove embarrassing when attempting to button your cuffs in public.

THE CHAIR SWIVEL

Gently rocking back and forth in your chair exercises the leg muscles as well as toning the torso. Make sure the chair is well-oiled so that it does not squeak. A squeaking chair can result in injury, particularly if others are sensitive to the noise.

THE FULL BODY STRETCH

This is a tricky maneuver that requires actually standing up. Rise to your feet, taking care to maintain your balance. Lift both arms over your head and stretch your entire body. Pretend you're reaching for the ceiling or doing something else that requires great height, such as kissing a giraffe. Once you've gotten out all the kinks, carefully return to your seat and relax all over. Repeat as necessary.

THE BUTTOCKS CLENCH

This often-overlooked exercise can combat the localized weight gain known scientifically as "chair spread." This exercise is particularly effective while playing video games that involve shooting monsters. It also occurs naturally when your boss *catches* you playing video games.

Practice these exercises daily and you'll soon find you've developed enough muscle tone that you're ready for more strenuous maneuvers, such as Preparing Lunch or Going Outside.

EVEN THE RAT RACE
MUST HAVE AN EXIT RAMP

Throughout the past century, prognosticators predicted that Americans would enjoy more leisure time. Technological advances would mean shorter workweeks, they said, leaving laborers free to frolic and muse.

Those forecasts turned out to be about as reliable as your brother-in-law. High-demand, high-stress jobs mean we're working more than ever. Leisure time remains as elusive as world peace.

Brace yourself. I'm going to throw some numbers at you now.

Americans labor more hours than workers in any other industrialized country. We clocked an average of 1,966 hours in 1997, up nearly 4 percent from 1,883 hours in 1980, according to a study by the International Labor Organization. That's nearly two full weeks more than workers in Japan, where average hours on the job dropped from 2,121 hours in 1980 to 1,889 in 1995. The French logged 1,656 hours in 1997 and the Germans worked 1,560. Those dynamos of productivity, the Norwegians and the Swedes, worked 1,399 hours and 1,552 hours, respectively.

A recent Roper Starch Worldwide Inc. poll of 2,000 Americans found that leisure hours have declined from 38.2 per week in 1993 to 35.3 in 1998.

In that same poll, commissioned by Hearst Magazines, respondents were asked what they would do with an extra hour or two per day. The No. 1 response was sleep, followed by spending time on a hobby, reading, exercising, doing nothing, watching TV, and making love. (How's that for priorities?)

For Americans who work at home, the situation is even more severe. Many of us feel a moral imperative to work, work, work, partly because our spouses bring home the real dough and partly because our work surrounds us all day. Along with profit-making work, there's housework, yardwork, laundry, and cooking. Throw a couple of kids into the equation, and it adds up to 12,000 hours a year. (Let's see the Japanese top that.)

Since a year has only 8,766 hours, at-home workers soon learn there's not enough time to do all the jobs and do them right. The only way to include any sort of leisure activity is to let some things fall by the wayside. Mopping, for instance.

To find time for leisure, you have to prioritize. I suggest making a list of the jobs you must accomplish each week. Rank them in order of importance. Then lose the list. That way, maybe you'll get lucky and forget some of the chores you'd planned to do. Or, you can squeeze leisure time into your workday. Use your lunch hour to exercise or pursue a hobby. Use time spent on hold to read a favorite novel. Peruse the newspaper while your computer reboots. Sleeping at your desk, I'm sorry to say, doesn't count.

However you do it, make time for yourself. For example, I skip out one night a week (while my wife bravely ferries our sons to Cub Scouts) to visit my best buddy. We play Scrabble and drink Cokes and eat M&Ms—a couple of wild and crazy guys— and try very hard not to think about the work we should be doing. It's true leisure time. And it's one activity that helps me keep my precarious grasp on sanity.

Follow my lead, you at-home workers. Get out of the house, get away from the piles of paperwork and dirty laundry. Plunge into doing nothing, at least for a few hours a week. It will make you a better worker and a better parent. But most important, it'll make you a better poll respondent. When the pollsters come calling, tell them your leisure hours are on the rise, that you're working less, and that you've never been happier.

If we all pull together, we can at least make it *look* as if we're not working all the time. Otherwise, Americans eventually will say they've had enough. We'll see a brain drain as we lose productive workers to other countries.

I'm considering Norway myself.

MAKE THE MOST OF THE OCCASIONAL DAY OFF

Weekends usually just mean more work for people who toil at home. Spouse and children go into a sloppy, who-cares-it's-the-weekend mode, and the spouse-in-charge becomes ever more harried, trying to keep the household together. And there's no way to keep up because we're outnumbered. All this, plus we try to pack in recreational activities, so our spouses won't discover we've become total drudges who've forgotten how to have fun.

This nonstop, seven-day-a-week workload is one reason it's so important for at-home workers to occasionally treat themselves to a real day off. Pack the kids off to Grandma's and let them wreck her house for a change. Ignore the clutter, dust, and dirty socks. Avoid the computer the telephone, and the fax machine. Take some time just for yourself, luxuriate in the lack of demands, get a massage, go to a movie, read undisturbed. Or just sit quietly, shell-shocked, not quite believing you have a day to yourself.

How best to spend a day alone? I've taken an informal poll of housespouses and have ranked the popularity of their suggestions. I offer them to you, as a public service, so you can make the most of those rare days of solitude:

1. Sleep.
2. Nap.
3. Drink beer.
4. Doze.
5. Sit in quiet repose, plotting how to get more days off.
6. Gardening (although this comes dangerously close to working).
7. Lounge by the pool.
8. Sleep by the pool.
9. Treat sunburn.
10. Go to the movies and pig out on popcorn.
11. Watch rented videos and pig out on microwave popcorn.
12. Purge.
13. Indulge in a bubble bath and hours of personal grooming.
14. Stare longingly into the mirror, wishing that grooming made a difference.
15. Go to a park, lie on your back in the soft grass, and count clouds. Awaken hours later to treat sunburn and insect bites.
16. Sit in the cool indoors and meditate. Try to ignore squeaky sound the air conditioner suddenly is making.
17. Read good books.
18. Read trashy books.
19. Thumb through magazines.
20. Thumb a ride to the next town so your family can't find you when they get back.

14.

AROUND THE CALENDAR,
OR
SCHOOL'S OUT *AGAIN?*

Like most newspaper types, I often write columns pegged to specific holidays or seasons. When you've got a fresh deadline every week, you take any hook you can find. Holidays and summer vacations are not just column fodder, however. They also offer a look at what *you* can expect as a work-at-home parent.

SUMMER

AH, SUMMER: NOW WHERE DID I PUT MY CHILDREN?

The end of the school year is a time of great rejoicing, a celebration of emancipation from homework, classwork, and science fair projects.

For the kids, that is. For parents, the end of school signals something quite different—a time of panic and despair. Our tax-payer-funded babysitters are closing for the summer. Now what the heck are we supposed to do?

Parents who work outside the home must find someplace to store their kids in the summer. Call it camp, call it day care, call it whatever you want, these parents must find someone to watch the children while they're at work. And, unless they have a relative nearby who'll do it for free, they can count on spending big bucks to keep the kids happily occupied.

For we who work at home, the child-care options are varied and flexible. Most of them, though, are aimed at allowing us to spend *less* time with our children. After a month of having kids shrieking and tearing through the house, an expensive day camp starts to seem like a pretty good idea.

Of course, by then it's too late. All the summer programs were completely filled back in, oh, February. If you've waited until summer actually begins to find a place for your children, you might as well forget it. You're stuck, trapped with your kids for the next three months.

Parents develop a range of coping strategies to deal with this annual home invasion. Maybe one of these models will work for you. Or, maybe having the little darlings at home all summer will send you scurrying back to a real job in an office, where children aren't allowed.

THE MARTHAS

Named after their patron saint, Martha Stewart, the Marthas are well-organized dynamos. They plan lots of activities for their homebound children. They stock supplies for creative art projects. They store toys in alphabetical order so the kids are never at a loss for playthings. They cook nutritious lunches. They get their children to help with interior-decorating projects. They go on elaborate, well-planned vacations. (Message to all you Marthas out there: the rest of us hate you.)

THE PARKERS

These parents specialize in parking their children at various places for an hour or two. This gives them a breather and helps them cope. Skillful Parkers do their research in advance, so they know which summer programs allow one-shot visitors and which malls have rent-a-cops patrolling for unaccompanied minors.

Other parents must beware the Parkers. One of their methods

is the so-called "play date," in which they successfully dump their kids at friends' homes. Non-Parkers have to learn to say no to play dates. Otherwise, you end up with entire herds of unwashed children in your home every day. And therein lies madness.

THE TORPORS

Most of us fall into this category, though we might not admit it. We go into a sort of hibernation when summer arrives. We hang around the house in our pajamas all day, stirred from sluggishness only to referee disputes between children. Our answer to every complaint about cabin fever: "Go outside and play."

I use a variation on this method. Any time my sons start driving me crazy, I put them to work. I see it as part of their education, a version of home economics. It's important that they learn to sweep, dust, and load a washing machine. Once they see the pattern, they tend to play quietly rather than risk being part of a work crew.

If this method fails to preserve my sanity, you might be hearing from me. I'll be calling about a "play date."

ROAD TRIPS:
TOO MUCH TOGETHERNESS

Summer is the time to pack up the family and drive across country on vacation. See the grand panoramas of America. Soak up history and culture at museums and national monuments. Spend meaningful time together. Fill those photo albums.

Had you going for a minute there, didn't I?

Let's face it. For most of us, traveling with our kids is a battle of wills. Children gag at the thought of a museum. They make faces at the camera. They wander off. They get bored. Seen one grand panorama, you've seen 'em all. The national monuments kids want have golden arches. All together now: "Are we there yet?"

My wife and I take our two sons across country to Arkansas

to see my relatives nearly every summer. More than nine hundred miles each way, through some of the most unspectacular country on God's Earth. Interstate 40 takes you through eastern New Mexico, which is almost scenic in a big, empty sort of way. Then there's the endlessly flat Texas panhandle and the whole rolling blah of Oklahoma.

People in that part of the world know they don't have much to offer. Their tourist attractions are big enough that you can marvel at them without stopping the car. The Cadillac Ranch near Amarillo. The World's Largest Cross in Groom, Texas. Oklahoma has a lakeside exit called Lotawatah Road (hilarious laughter from the kids), and in Texas there's one called Arnot Road ("Are, too!"). That's about it. In Oklahoma, I always look for a town called Allright, OK, because that's what we parents keep saying, but I haven't found it yet.

We're veterans at these pilgrimages. We know to take plenty of toys and books. We know to keep lots of snacks hidden in the car. We know to stop overnight in a motel with an indoor pool. We even stock the car with children's music on cassette. Of course, that's hard on the adults. After a dozen listens to Bob Dylan croaking "This Old Man" or chirpy folksingers giving us "Little Bunny Fou-Fou," we're pulling out our hair. Making up new lyrics helps. One song strings together all the parts of the body by funny names—"smell-sniffer" and "soup-strainer" and the like. My wife and I sing a version that goes: "nosepicker, backstabber, bootlicker, pants-dropper . . ." The boys don't understand why we're laughing up in the front seat.

As the kids get older, each trip gets a little easier. The older boy simply reads one book after another, never looking up until we reach our destination. The younger one plays with his plastic superheroes and handheld video games, sleeps and, twice an hour or so, says, "How much longer 'til we get there?"

We travel eight hours a day. On the most recent trip, our younger son was good for about seven hours, then his patience wore out and he started getting into trouble.

During the last hour of our trip home, when we could see

Albuquerque's mountains, the Sandias, looming up ahead, he amused himself by removing his shoes and tossing his smelly socks at my head. My wife was driving, so he left her alone. But the shotgun-seat passenger makes a heck of a target. Knowing we were in that deadly last hour and trying to be the good-natured dad, I tossed them back. Oh, that was so funny we had to do it again. About the ninth time a stinky sock hit me in the head, I wheeled on him and, laughing villainously, rubbed it all over his nose, saying, "How do *you* like that smell? Hah?"

His reply: "Smells like French fries!"

By that time, everything in the car smelled like French fries.

So, as your summer driving vacation nears, remember this advice: lots of food, lots of distractions, regular exercise breaks. And keep their socks in the trunk.

SUMMERTIME, AND THE GRILLING IS GREASY

Any fool can hurt himself in a modern kitchen, but to really get some third-degree burns, you need a barbecue grill.

Summertime is cookout season. Time to go out in the yard, stand under the broiling sun, and char some artery-clogging meat. Create a mushroom cloud of oily smoke that'll have your neighbors dialing 911. Enjoy the sizzle of spattering grease hitting your howling dinner guests.

For eons now, since the day our humble ancestors discovered fire, people have been using open flames to turn simple animal flesh into crunchy, bleeding, chew-proof repasts. Cavemen squatted around fires on the ground, but we've come far since then. Now we have barbecue grills, which stand on legs, putting the flames even closer to your face and other anatomical regions that react poorly to burning.

The barbecue grill was invented by the ancient Romans. In fact, the word "barbecue" comes from the Latin "barbecus," which translates to "my apron is on fire." Those fun-loving

Romans knew that nothing makes a meal more enjoyable than watching the host prance around in flames.

In contemporary times, cookouts have become synonymous with summer, as American as apple pie, fireworks, and paper plates. When it's already a hundred degrees outside, why not go out and start a big, hot fire? Heatstroke is a good excuse for steaks that are poorly cooked.

Outdoor grilling has become the province of men. Big, sweaty guys who wouldn't be caught dead whipping up something in the kitchen will push others out of the way to get to a barbecue grill. Why? Because of the element of risk involved. There's something *manly* about poking and prodding among roaring blazes. Men bring their charred offerings to the table, their chests puffed out, the hair singed off their arms, and they feel like they've proven something. They've proven they can produce a meal without setting the lawn on fire—this time.

At our house, my wife has taken over the grilling chores. It's part of our whole role-reversal thing, plus it gives her the opportunity to cook burgers that don't come out like hockey pucks. This resolves a conflict that has plagued us through eighteen years of married life: I like meat well-done to the point of inedibility, she wants rare, rare, rare. Her idea of cooking a steak is to show an unlit match to a live cow.

I don't feel usurped now that she's the one sweating over the grill. Better for me to sit in a lawn chair a safe distance away, swilling beer, and offering advice such as: "Hon, your hair's on fire."

There may be those among you who haven't yet savored the joys of cooking outdoors. What follows is advice on properly using a grill. Take this advice seriously. I'm a barbecue veteran, and I've got the scars to prove it.

CHOOSING A GRILL

Barbecue grills come in a vast array of sizes and styles, from the big Cadillac models with side burners and aloe vera plants, down to the lowly "hibachi" (from the Japanese for "my kimono's on fire"). When selecting your grill, the main question will be: charcoal or gas? Gas grills are easier to use, but they're essentially just outdoor stoves. Charcoal gives meat a wonderful smoky flavor, and the risk is high. Ask any impatient cook who's decided a little more charcoal starter should be spritzed onto the sputtering coals. Nothing's as satisfying as the sudden *whoompf* of flames twenty feet high.

CLEANING YOUR GRILL

You're supposed to clean them? Haha, just kidding. A wire brush does a nice job of removing ash and blackened meat bits. Don't worry about cleaning the outside of the grill. Just leave it outdoors over the winter and let Mother Nature do the work. Once it rusts out, it's time to get a new one.

GRILL SAFETY

Surely it's clear by now that "safe grilling" is an oxymoron. You want safe, you should go to a restaurant. Tell the waiter you want your steak just like you eat them at home: black on the outside, bloody on the inside, and covered in ashes and bugs. While you're at it, see if you can get him to set his apron on fire.

TAN MY HIDE—
IT'S SWIMMING TIME

A perceptive reporter I know once did an article on stay-at-home dads and came away with this observation: all the men had tanned feet.

I was welcomed into their ranks recently when a house guest arrived and said, before she'd even come indoors, "Look! Even your toes are tanned!"

Every summer, I get a suntan because I'm a stay-at-home parent. In the past, I spent all my time working and writing, and you can't get a tan from the glow of a computer monitor. But with my sons home from school for the summer, I quickly discovered the pool was the best place to spend long, hot afternoons.

Swimming is a way to channel the boundless energy of children. It wears them out for bedtime. It gives them a chance to practice their negligible social skills on other kids. And it gives me a chance to rest and soak up some rays.

Tanning doesn't come easy to people of Anglo-Germanic origin. We're melanin-challenged, our natural skin tone a shade I call Moby Dick white. So we slather on the sunscreen—SPF 600, I think it is—for protection from the blistering New Mexico sun. In the tiniest of increments, we change to a life-like color. Not bronze, exactly, but darker than the zombies in *Night of the Living Dead*.

We go to the pool every other day, taking the day off in between to let sun-hot skin cool. On weekdays, I'm often the only representative of the species Big, Hairy Dad on the premises. Sometimes I catch the moms eyeing me suspiciously, probably wondering why I'm not at a real job during office hours. Those of us who work at home know office hours are whenever you can get them—early in the morning, late at night, whenever the kids are asleep or otherwise occupied. Three hours at the pool is just an extended coffee break.

My personality changes at the pool. A normally modest sort who wouldn't dream of jiggling around shirtless while, say, mowing the lawn, I strip down to my trunks and beach myself on the nearest lounge chair without a thought to whether anyone's watching. I hide behind sunglasses and a fat book. I'm usually vain about my hair, but I don't even care as it dries into an arrangement that would make a porcupine proud.

Even my name changes. I become "Watchthisdaddy." My sons are bold, doing cannonballs off the diving board, initiating splash fights, and leaping into the deep end. Aquatic daredevils to the end, as long as they have "Watchthisdaddy" as an audience.

It's not just my kids, either. "Watch this!" is part of the everyday cacophony of the swimming pool, a steady background noise of squeals, shouts, splashes, and shrieking lifeguard whistles. Sometimes, as I'm dropping off to sleep at night, I can still hear, ringing in my ears: "Marco! Polo! Marco! Polo!"

We come home from the pool reeking of sunscreen and chlorine, hang damp towels and swimsuits on the coat rack, and repair immediately to the kitchen. What is it about swimming that makes you voracious? It can't be simply the burning of calories through exercise. Often, I don't swim enough to even breathe hard. But by the time I get home, I'm ready to gobble my way through the fridge like the shark in *Jaws*. It shows, of course. I gain weight during the summer. I try not to think about how I look in my swim trunks, though the phrase "Thar he blows!" echoes in my head. And I tell myself: it's just more to tan.

FALL

IT'S HALLOWEEN: UNLEASH THE NINJAS

My younger son brought home a paper from school last October that went like this: "For Halloween, I want to wear a costume like a (blank)." My son had written in "ninja."

This made me gnash my teeth. Not because I have anything against ninjas. I'm sure they're perfectly nice people, once you get past all the kicking, swordplay, and screaming "hee-yah!" as they eviscerate each other. No, I've got nothing against ninjas and I hope all you ninjas out there take note of this.

And it's not because I don't want my kids wearing Halloween costumes that portray violent characters. Children—especially boys—are violent little creatures by nature and I've given up on trying to change that. I made that decision years ago, when one of them was still eating in a high-chair. As I approached, he held up a cracker, perfectly chewed into the shape of a pistol, and said, "Bang!" I knew then that I and my liberal, anti-gun tendencies were whipped.

No, the reason I'm irked by "ninja" as a job description for a trick-or-treater is that I'd thought we had our Halloween costuming plans all set, and ninjas didn't figure into it.

My wife and my older son had picked up these great masks at a flea market. They're whole-head masks, made of rubber, depicting old-man faces, complete with wrinkles, blemishes, and various discolorations. Each bald head sports a halo of long, white, fake hair. The first time my kids walked into the room wearing these masks, it startled the bejeebees out of me. I thought we'd been invaded by retired Munchkins. Once the shock wore off, though, I could see these masks were the basis for perfect Halloween costumes. Wear them with overalls and you're an ancient farmer. Wear them with a bathrobe and you're a wizard. Wear them with pants hitched up to your armpits, and you're somebody's grandpa.

It was a relief, having Halloween all planned, but still leaving room for the all-important, last-minute improvisation.

See, at our house, the kids tend to be capricious about their costumes. They change their minds as frequently as most of us change our underwear. In fact, I wish I could get them to change their own underwear as often.

It starts around October 1, when Halloween is still a distant Jack-o'-lantern glow on the horizon. The boys plunge into a big box of costumes and old clothes and begin mixing and matching the possibilities. They come into the living room, done up head to toe, and boldly announce that *this* combination is their final selection for Halloween. We smile and nod, happy in the knowledge that that's been sorted out and pleased with their inventiveness. Then, a day or two later, they appear in completely different outfits. This goes on for the whole month. By the time Halloween actually arrives, they're sick of all of their options and we have to do a mad scramble to get them into some costume, any costume, so the neighbors will fork over the candy.

One year, we did face painting at the last minute. One kid was a werewolf (brown face) and the other was a pumpkin (orange face). Under the neighbors' porch lights, both boys looked as if they'd rolled in mud.

Another time, they were tuxedoed vampires, but they couldn't say "Trick or treat" without first removing their plastic fangs. Without the teeth, they looked like butlers. Another year, they wore uniforms that vaguely suggested *Star Trek*, along with plastic swords. When people asked what they were supposed to be, they rolled their eyes and said, "Space Ninjas," as if any fool could see that.

But this particular Halloween, I was determined that they'd wear those little-old-man masks, no matter what. I'd worked hard, keeping those masks hidden away so the dog wouldn't shred them. I wanted all that effort to pay off.

We ended up dressing the boys in ninja costumes and the old-man masks. When the neighbors asked what they were supposed to be, my boys rolled their eyes, sighed exasperatedly, and replied, "Retirement-home ninjas."

LET'S ALL GIVE THANKS
FOR HANDI-WIPES

Thanksgiving is the time to look back upon the past year and recognize that our children have no table manners.

Yes, Thanksgiving is a time for warm family gatherings and huge, gluttonous turkey dinners, where our children invariably will embarrass the heck out of us in front of our doting relatives. It's a time for unrestrained burping, wandering off from the table, drumming silverware, and yes, God help us, food fights.

The bounteous feast we traditionally prepare at Thanksgiving is too much temptation for kids. All those heaping mounds of abundance simply demand that some of it become airborne. And all the grown-ups on hand mean plenty of attention when a child misbehaves.

How does this happen? We parents work throughout the year, trying to impress upon our children the importance of chewing with one's mouth closed, only to have them act like barbarians as soon as everyone is seated for the big dining event of the year. They giggle and squirm while someone says grace. Then it's "gimme some turkey" and "oops, I dropped it on the carpet" and "play ball!" with the dinner rolls.

After much study, I've concluded that the problem is simply

that we, as parents, are miserable failures when it comes to teaching manners. Perhaps it's that we don't set good examples at home, only using good manners when dining in public. Perhaps we don't use good teaching methods—cuffing a kid on the back of the head only makes him choke. And perhaps we ourselves simply don't understand table manners well enough to pass them along to the next generation.

Here, then, is the traditional Turkey Day Table Manners' Quiz. Use it to determine whether you measure up as a parent.

Question: The utensil to the immediate right of the dinner plate is a:
(A) Fork
(B) Spoon
(c) Plastic "spork" left over from the last trip to Kentucky Fried Chicken
(D) What's a "utensil?"

Question: The proper response when one burps loudly at the table is:
(A) "Excuse me."
(B) "Oh, my. I'm terribly sorry."
(c) "Who belched?"
(D) "Good one!"

Question: It's traditional at Thanksgiving that the turkey be carved by:
(A) The family patriarch
(B) The family matriarch
(c) Whoever's quickest with a knife.
(D) "Just tear off a piece with your bare hands."

Question: When requesting a portion of turkey, one should say:
(A) "White meat, please."
(B) "Dark meat for me, please."

(c) "Ugh, not that part. Put that back."

(d) "Boy, this turkey sure looks *dry.*"

Question: Cranberry sauce should be eaten with a:

(A) Fork

(B) Spoon

(c) Ten-foot pole

(D) You're supposed to *eat* it?

Question: If one spills one's drink at the table, one should:

(A) Apologize and wait for the host to clean up the mess.

(B) Leap up and use your napkin to clean it up yourself.

(c) Say, "Aw, damn, not *again!*"

(D) Laugh hysterically.

Question: If place cards are used at the table, the polite guest should:

(A) Gracefully sit where assigned, even if it means you're beside Uncle Claude, whose nose whistles when he chews.

(B) Switch the cards so someone else must sit next to Uncle Claude.

(c) Remove all the cards and shout, "It's time for some spontaneity around here!"

(D) Sit at the "kiddie table."

Question: If a food fight erupts, a responsible adult will:

(A) Stop it immediately and scold the perpetrators.

(B) Declare a truce and clean up the mess.

(c) Demand concessions from the enemy under threat of more ballistic peas.

(D) Refuse to hurl silverware because someone could be hurt.

If you look over your answers, you'll likely see the reason your children always misbehave at Thanksgiving dinner. We parents have only ourselves to blame.

WINTER

LET THE THERMOSTAT WARS BEGIN!

Welcome to winter, the Official Season of Lost Gloves.

As cold weather settles over the nation, we're all indoors more, getting on each other's nerves. We must wear more clothing to brave the elements. Driving and walking outdoors take on an air of ice-slick danger. Winter should be safe and happy, so I've developed the following Winter Survival Guide to help you weather the months ahead.

CABIN FEVER

Being shut up in a cozy house seems romantic when portrayed on TV—flames dancing in the fireplace, frost on the windows, fuzzy slippers, and candlelight. But let's face it, unless you're on an all-expenses-paid honeymoon in Aspen, life indoors just isn't that pleasant, especially if children are around. A few days cooped up with kids will make you long for summer, when "Go outside" worked as a remedy for frayed nerves.

Even happily married, child-free couples start to annoy each other if they're trapped together indoors. An innocent habit, such as gum-cracking, mindless sniffing, or adjusting the thermostat every few minutes, easy to ignore when you're outside a lot, becomes unbearably grating when you're indoors together for days on end. Pretty soon, homicide starts to look like a viable solution.

How to cope with cabin fever? Brandy seems to have medicinal qualities (why do you think those St. Bernards carry it around in the Alps?) and hot cocoa can soothe. But the best treatment remains time alone. You and your spouse should occupy opposite ends of the house as much as possible. And kids can still be forced to go outside if you wrap them in enough outer-garments.

BUNDLING UP

When it gets really cold outside, responsible parents provide their children with the following: long underwear, jeans or ski pants, two pairs of socks, waterproof shoes, T-shirt, sweatshirt, flannel shirt, anorak, heavy coat, gloves or mittens, a woolly scarf, and a warm hat. Each of these items will be greeted by objections from the children, who see nothing wrong with dressing like Tarzan when it's snowing. Parents should calmly ignore the complaints and apply each layer as carefully as if it were a coat of paint. By the time you're done, you won't be able to tell whether there's a child inside all those garments. If the child can move freely, he's probably not wearing enough clothes.

The only exception to child clothing complaints: kids want the biggest, bulkiest ski gloves they can possibly find, because those are the kind that shoots lasers.

SCHEDULING

Even a quick trip to the convenience store becomes an Arctic expedition during bad weather. If the kids are going with you, allow an extra thirty minutes for preparation and protests. Slick roads slow you down, so allow for that in your daily schedule. And, unexpected storms can bring the whole city to a halt. In fact, if you've got anywhere to go between now and Christmas, you'd better get started now.

HOUSEWORK

If you must spend so much time indoors, at least it can be in an orderly environment. But, naturally, winter presents its own set of problems here, too. All those clothes mentioned earlier? They end up on the floor. So you won't need to exercise much during the winter. You'll be doing toe-touches all day long, bending over to pick up mittens and mufflers.

This problem is compounded by the fact that winter occurs during basketball season. Nothing can be put away normally. Every item can be discarded only in the following manner: "He shoots! He scores!" If you, the parent, hear "He shoots!" followed by silence, then you know that's another item you'll be picking up later.

All those clothes must be kept clean. Expect your weekly laundry load to double.

Another problem: All the snow/ice/sludge/mud tracked into the house. Ignore this at your peril. Soon, the footing inside won't be any safer than the icy sidewalks outside.

PETS

Keep them in the house with you as much as possible. Otherwise, they'll go missing and you'll have a big surprise when the snowdrifts melt.

There you have it. If you follow this advice, you can survive the coming winter and all its hazards. And remember, spring is only eighteen months away.

CHRISTMAS COMES BUT ONCE A YEAR, BUT BEEPING TOYS ARE FOREVER

Christmas is the season of gift-giving, a time of joy and peace and so much warmth that you can roast your chestnuts if you're not careful. Only one phrase adequately sums up the holiday spirit for parents everywhere: "Batteries not included."

That's right, ladies and ye merry gentlemen. No matter how well you've planned, somewhere in that pile of gilt-wrapped gifts is a toy that will sit inert on Christmas morning because it doesn't have batteries. Even if you took special pains to avoid battery-powered toys (and, boy, the folks at Eveready hate to hear that), some relative has sent your children a race car, a laser gun, or a virtual pet that needs forty-seven AAA batteries.

If you look in every drawer in your house, under the seats of your car, and in your neighbors' homes, you won't come up with enough batteries to make this gizmo go. You'll think about stealing the batteries out of the TV remote, just to get the kid to stop wailing over a toy that is essentially a paperweight.

(A word of advice: don't rob from the remote. Some things

are sacrosanct. And there's a lot of televised football during the holidays.)

When our children were younger, we followed the wisdom of the experts who say simple toys encourage children to use their imaginations. These experts recommend versatile playthings, like Lincoln Logs and Tinkertoy and Lego. Noisy, battery-powered toys that only do one thing are *verboten* because children quickly become bored with them. This is good advice, but there are two problems the so-called experts don't address.

1. Lincoln Logs and Lego don't pick themselves up when the kids are done with them. They pose hazards to bare feet and eventually become dog kibble.
2. Grandparents.

No matter how well-intentioned the parents, grandparents are the wild card. They'll buy anything, the louder and more annoying, the better. Grandparents know they're not the ones who'll be around when the kids crash the remote-control fire truck with "real live siren howl" into the walls again and again. No, it'll be the parents who are awake in the middle of the night, stealthily removing the batteries to give their frayed nerves a break.

At our house, it all began with a little pink dog. When our older (and, at that time, only) son was two years old, my parents shipped him a fuzzy pink dog that ran on, as I recall, eighty-three batteries. The dog would walk forward, rear up on its hind legs, open its mouth and go "yap, yap, yap." Then it would start the process all over again. Our son loved this toy more than any of the educational toys we purchased. He ran it day and night— "yap, yap, yap"—until I thought my head would explode.

That one took care of itself. My son decided the pink dog needed a bath, so he dumped it in the toilet. We cleaned the dog, dried it, and (against our better judgment) put in new batteries. But after its swirling swim, the dog was mute. It still would walk, rear up, and its little mouth would open and close, but the only sound was the grinding of its gears. Its yapper was ruined forever. I secretly offered up prayers of thanks every time I laid eyes on the dog.

After this adventure, we encouraged my parents to avoid such toys. Their reply? A diabolical "heh-heh-heh."

Every year, they send at least one gift that needs many batteries and makes a variety of whizbang noises you can hear all over the house.

The topper was the Christmas they gave both sons police cars that not only ran around, sirens blaring, but would stop occasionally, raise up on a hidden pedestal, sprout wings and whirl in place, screaming all the while. It was as if your friendly neighborhood patrol car had mated with the Batmobile.

Fortunately, the experts are right. After a week or two, the kids lose interest in these toys and go back to their make-believe world, where they provide their own screaming. Or, the batteries die.

Take my advice: You, too, can "forget" to buy new batteries until these gadgets end up dead and silent in the bottom of the toy-box.

If that doesn't work, there's always the toilet.

SPRING

SPRING TRAINING: "ALMOST" IS GOOD ENOUGH

When my two sons were younger, I taught them to swing a bat at a plastic ball tossed underhand. When they whiffed, which was often, they would call out "Almost!"

Not "oops," "darn," or "never again," which would have signaled frustration, but "almost." They almost hit it, and they were ready to try again. If they missed again, so what? As long as they swung the bat, as long as they made an effort, they had almost succeeded.

I remember smiling every time they said it, and reminding myself that this was a good philosophy for any effort. Do your best, and see how it turns out. "Almost" keeps you from giving up or stomping off in anger or blaming the pitcher or the coach. There's an optimism attached to "almost" that's missing from most other words. "Almost" means not yet, but I'm still trying.

Grown-ups use "almost," though mostly to buy time or to qualify answers when we're uncertain. What do we say when asked if we're done with a task? "Almost." How do we answer when asked if we'll meet a looming deadline? "Almost." What do we think when someone calls the boss a "perfect idiot?" We think "almost" because nobody's perfect.

Most of us know the difference between a job well done and one done well enough. That gray area in between is where "almost" lives. We all want to excel, but let's face it, the closest most of us come is "almost." Why chew your lips off trying to be the very best when "almost" is close enough for jazz?

The "almost" approach takes the pressure off. And it leaves the door open for another attempt. How often have you done all you can, working long hours and giving yourself a big fat headache, only to find that the results weren't quite what your superiors had in mind? There's no sense trying to tell them about "almost," but "almost" can be a cushion to collapse upon when you think you can't take any more.

I'm not endorsing goldbricking or lollygagging. I think you should try your best. But striving for perfection comes with a high price: ulcers, migraines, depression, anger, impatience, spoiled relationships, and the various escape hatches seemingly offered by drugs, drink, or other bad habits. All because you weren't perfect, even if you "almost" made it.

We should embrace "almost." Let it soothe us. Let it ease that impatient hustle-bustle that plagues our lives. We all know we can't be perfect at every task, all the time. But if we've done the best we can under the circumstances, then "almost" is probably good enough.

It's a hard lesson to learn. Americans are competitive strivers. Society demands that we go full tilt all the time, trying to get ahead, to make a buck, to outdo our coworkers. Outside of work, we struggle to have the cleanest house, the slimmest thighs, the funniest jokes, or the lowest golf scores.

The pressure builds as we push for perfection. The result? All the fun goes out of the tasks. It's possible to enjoy the most mundane chore if you slow down and pay attention. But we all go too fast, trying to get it over with so we can move on to the next thing. If we don't stop to smell the roses, the only odors we get are sweat and fertilizer.

I spent many years working for newspapers, where the daily grind consists of going as fast as you can without making a single mistake. These days, I'm trying to slow down, to savor the work, to stay optimistic about how it will all turn out.

Am I succeeding?

Almost.

15.

CONCLUSIONS,

OR,

IS IT TIME TO UPDATE MY RÉSUMÉ?

I guess it's clear by now that working at home isn't for everyone. It's one of those situations that looks great until you actually try it—much like parenthood.

Even those of us who've managed to find the secret rhythm of household happiness sometimes question whether we made a mistake climbing onto the Daddy Track. These questions usually arise during times of crisis, such as when a child is projectile vomiting into a toilet that won't flush. Or when credit card companies send Final Notices.

No problem, you might say. If it doesn't work out, I'll just go back to a real job. But it's not as simple as that. For one thing, working at home spoils you. Could you really face coworkers, office politics, and some boss chewing on your neck all day after enjoying the freedom of life at home? For another, all those neck-chewers out there in the corporate world will have forgotten you ever existed.

Once you've worked at home for a while, you're locked in. (I mean that figuratively, though I'm sure some stay-at-home spouses are literally locked in their home offices until they get some work done.) You're committed to rearing the children, keeping the house and, oh by the way, getting some of your own work done. Returning to the suit-and-tie world would mean locating child care, a cleaning service, and getting new tires on the car for that daily commute. Who can afford all that? You'd have to juggle your whole life. And your working spouse, who's been so understanding (ha, ha!) about your need to stay home, won't be too pleased to hear you want to turn everything upside down all over again.

But say you've overcome your spouse's objections (or she's kicked you out of the house) and you're determined to go out there and get a regular job. How to explain the gap in your résumé? Will you have the paperwork to quantify what you've been doing since you bailed out? I'm here to tell you, potential employers won't care that you've successfully survived working at home. They won't care that you did laundry, made beds, and mastered the weed-whacker. And they won't see that tending a couple of children equates to managing your own firm, not unless you had the foresight to name your kids Dot and Com.

Employers will be suspicious. They'll wonder whether you had some kind of mental breakdown that led you to stay home. They'll suspect you're too much of a free spirit to toe the company line. They'll figure that some failure of personality or business acumen prompted you to come crawling back to the corporate world.

And even if they understand why you left and why you want to return, they'll be jealous of the time that you had away. No doubt it's just the sort of "early retirement" they've always dreamed of, but have been unable to pull off themselves. Of course, they only believe that a home business equates to retirement because they've never tried it. Most people think of working at home and it translates into "working on my tan."

We who are out in the trenches of the home front know that we've never worked harder for less pay. We know that your standard eight hours in an office is nothing compared to the twenty-four-hour-a-day, high-stress, high-demand life of a work-at-home parent. We know that sinking feeling you get when you decapitate a sprinkler head with the lawn mower or when you hear a mysterious ticking sound somewhere in the house.

Let's face it, when most of us jettisoned a normal career in